The World's Funniest

LAWYER JOKES

The World's Funniest

LAWYER JOKES

A CASELOAD OF JURISPRUDENTIAL JESTS

STEVEN D. PRICE

Skyhorse Publishing

Skyhorse Publishing books may be purchased in bulk at special discounts for sales promotion, corporate gifts, fund-raising, or educational purposes. Special editions can also be created to specifications. For details, contact the Special Sales Department, Skyhorse Publishing, 307 West 36th Street, 11th Floor, New York, NY 10018 or info@skyhorsepublishing.com.

Skyhorse® and Skyhorse Publishing® are registered trademarks of Skyhorse Publishing, Inc.®, a Delaware corporation.

www.skyhorsepublishing.com

10 9 8 7 6 5 4 3 2 1

Library of Congress Cataloging-in-Publication Data

The world's funniest lawyer jokes : a caseload of jurisprudential jests / [collected] by Steven D. Price.
    p. cm.
  ISBN 978-1-61608-254-3 (pbk. : alk. paper)
  1. Lawyers--Humor. 2. Law--Humor. 3. Law--Anecdotes. I. Price, Steven D.
  PN6231.L4W67 2011
  818'.6020803554--dc22

                                2010043231

Printed in China

Contents

Introduction   vii

Acknowledgments   xi

CHAPTER ONE
"HOW ABOUT A LAWYER FOR MY 'GATOR?   3

CHAPTER TWO
ASKED AND ANSWERED   107

CHAPTER THREE
HERE COMES THE JUDGE . . .   141

CHAPTER FOUR
"WOE UNTO YE ALSO, YE LAWYERS"   159

CHAPTER FIVE
TRIALS AND TRIBULATIONS   191

CHAPTER SIX
SLIDING DOWN A BARRISTER   221

Introduction

WITH THE POSSIBLE EXCEPTION of "Yo' Mama," no identifiable group has been the butt of more jokes than lawyers, so let's begin this compendium of forensic funniness with an inquiry about why that is so.

The most convincing explanation came from a lawyer chum who pointed out that most people's only lifetime contact with the law is with regard to a divorce, a contested will, a minor (or perhaps a major) criminal charge or violation, a personal injury case, and/or a mortgage foreclosure. Those sorts of contacts will not leave you with a favorable impression of lawyers, especially where contingency fees strike the client as astronomical. Moreover, most people see lawyers as benefiting from others' misery.

Another friend's explanation deserves to be repeated verbatim: "The best lawyerly comment I can remember came from our East Tennessee town's Spit-and-Whittle Corner, where countrymen like my grandfather and my great-uncle Flea sat on benches producing cedar shavings, tobacco juice, and a vast array of opinions, one of which was about lawyers. (I'm paraphrasing now, as the eavesdropped commentary dates back 50 years to a time when I lacked the context for identifying countrymen's commentary as folklore, and not as pearls of wisdom from deep-thinking philosophers. Though, on reflection, maybe I identified it correctly on the first go-round.)

"Lawyers is just people paid to lie, is all. You go into any schoolroom, and you figure out who the biggest liar is, and ten to one he'll grow up to be a lawyer."

"Or a politician."

"T'hell's the difference?"

"Politicians is lawyers who don't lie good enough, and so have to sell at a discount."

"Well I'll tell you what I know about lawyers, and that's there ain't never one around unless you don't need one."

"Yonder goes one now."

"Hell, he ain't no lawyer. He's a judge."

"T'hell's the difference?"

"Judges is lawyers who've heard so much lying they got so's they can spy out the truth."

Cobbling together this collection, I came across a wide variety of anti-lawyer jokes. Some are admittedly pretty dopey, although enough people thought them worth passing along or else they would have disappeared; hence, why they appear here. Others, and many more so, display a scintilla or more of cleverness and originality. And lots more are laugh-out-loud funny. In addition to anti-lawyer jokes, I included examples of forensic wit and, in rarer instances, wisdom.

Divided into six chapters the book begins with "How About A Lawyer For My 'gator?"—the punchline of one of the jokes—and contains what the world has come to think of—and swap—as lawyer jokes. "Asked And Answered" are in question-and-answer or one-liner form. "Here Comes The Judge" focuses on adjudicators and others on the bench. "Woe Unto Ye Also, Ye Lawyers" (the chapter titles comes from the New Testament's Luke, Chapter 11) contains quotations from literature and other sources. "Trials And Tribulations" describe farfetched-but-true lawsuits, while "Sliding Down A Barrister" (a line by Dorothy Parker) concludes with an assortment of lawyerly anecdotes.

As happened after I finished my other books of quotations and pre-told tales, people asked which entry is my favorite. Far and away, the cleverest item that I came across was this exchange:

Joseph Choate once opposed an attorney from Westchester County (a wealthy residential area north of New York City) in a lawsuit in New York. The attorney, in a feeble attempt to belittle Choate, warned the jury not to be taken in by his colleague's "Chesterfieldian urbanity."

Choate, summing up his own arguments, in turn urged the jury not to be taken in by his opponent's "Westchesterfieldian suburbanity."

Not far behind is:

A junior partner in a law firm was sent to the state capital to represent a long-term client accused of robbery. After days of trial, the case was won, the client acquitted and released.

Excited about his success, the attorney e-mailed the firm: "Justice prevailed."

The senior partner sent his reply one second later, "Appeal immediately."

Although it's largely irrelevant, I might admit in the interest of full disclosure that I'm a law school graduate, so I had something of a vested (as in three-piece lawyer suit) interest in taking on this project. I restrained myself, however, from including any of my law school or bar exam answers, even though those who graded my papers most likely looked at what I wrote and exclaimed, "he must be joking!"

Ladies and gentlemen of the reading jury, enjoy!

Steven D. Price
September, 2010

Acknowledgments

A LOW BOW IN THE direction of lawyer friends Bob Abraham, Tony Ard, Neal Goldman, John Sands, Joan Fine, Lee Weisel, and Jack Hagele, and civilians Jim Babb, Norman Fine, Mike Cohen, Richard Liebmann-Smith, and Rich Goldman for their counsel, enthusiasm, and humor.

Thanks too to publisher-lawyer Tony Lyons for the chance to do this book.

The World's Funniest

LAWYER JOKES

CHAPTER ONE

"How About a Lawyer for My 'Gator?"

— A BRIEFCASE LOAD OF JOKES

THERE WAS A TERRIBLE accident at a railroad crossing; a train smashed into a car and pushed it nearly four hundred yards down the track. Though no one was killed, the driver of the car took the train company to court.

At the trial, the engineer insisted that he had given the driver ample warning by waving his lantern back and forth for nearly a minute. He even stood and convincingly demonstrated how he'd done it. The court believed his story, and the suit was dismissed.

"Congratulations," the lawyer said to the engineer when it was over. "You did superbly under cross-examination."

"Thanks," he said, "but he sure had me worried."

"How's that?" the lawyer asked.

"I was afraid he was going to ask if the lantern was lit."

~✦~

A man died and was taken to Hell. As he passed sulfurous pits and shrieking sinners, he saw a man he recognized as a lawyer snuggling up to a beautiful woman.

"That's unfair !" he cried. "I have to roast for all eternity, and that lawyer gets to spend it with a beautiful woman."

"Quiet!" barked the devil, "Who are you to question that woman's punishment?"

~♦~

A defendant who had pleaded not guilty saw the jury that had been empanelled and announced that he was changing his plea to guilty. When the judge asked why, the defendant pointed to the eight women and four men in the jury box. "When I pleaded 'not guilty,' I didn't know women would be on the jury. Judge, I can't fool even one woman, so I know I can't fool eight of them."

~♦~

Three lawyers and three MBAs are traveling by train to a conference. At the station, the MBAs each buy tickets and watch as the three lawyers buy only a single ticket

"How are three people going to travel on only one ticket?" asks an MBA.

"Watch and you'll see," answers one of the lawyers.

They all board the train. The MBAs take their respective seats but all three lawyers cram into a restroom and close the door behind them. Shortly after the train departs, the conductor comes around collecting tickets. He knocks on the restroom door and says, "Ticket, please."

The door opens just a crack and a single arm emerges with a ticket in hand. The conductor takes it and moves on.

The MBAs agreed it was quite a clever idea. So after the conference, the MBAs decide to copy the lawyers on the return trip and save some money. When they get to the station, they buy a single ticket for the return trip. To their astonishment, the lawyers don't buy any tickets at all.

"How are you going to travel without a ticket?" asked one perplexed MBA.

"Watch and you'll see," answers a lawyer.

When they board the train the three MBAs cram into a restroom and the three lawyers cram into another one nearby. The train departs.

Shortly afterward, one of the lawyers leaves his restroom and walks over to the restroom where the MBAs are hiding. He knocks on the door and says, "Ticket, please."

~+~

A woman and her little girl were visiting the grave of the little girl's grandmother. On their way through the cemetery back to the car, the little girl asked, "Mommy, do they ever bury two people in the same grave?"

"Of course not, dear," replied the mother. "Why would you think that?"

"The tombstone back there said, 'Here lies a lawyer and an honest man.'"

~ ✦ ~

The madam opened the brothel door to see a rather dignified, well-dressed, good-looking man in his late 40s or early 50s. "Can I help you?" she asked.

"I want to see Susan," the man replied.

"Sir, Susan is one of our most expensive ladies. Perhaps you would prefer someone else," said the madam.

"No, I must see Susan," was the man's reply.

Just then, Susan appeared and announced to the man that she charged $2,000 an hour. Without hesitation, the man pulled out twenty one-hundred dollar bills and gave them to Susan and they went upstairs. After an hour, the man calmly left.

The next night the same man appeared again, demanding to see Susan. Susan explained that no one had ever come back two nights in a row as she was too expensive and there were no discounts. The price was still $2,000. Again the man pulled out the money, gave it to Susan and they went upstairs. After an hour, he left.

The following night the man was there again. Everyone was astounded that he had come for the third consecutive night, but he paid Susan and they went upstairs. After their session, Susan said to the man. "No one has ever used my services three nights in a row. Where are you from?"

The man replied, "California."

"Really?" she said. "I have family in California."

"I know," the man said. "Your aunt died and I am your cousin's lawyer. She instructed me to give you your $6,000 inheritance."

∼✦∼

Satan was complaining bitterly to God, "You made the world so that it was not fair, and you made it so that most people would have to struggle every day, fight against their innate wishes and desires, and deal with all sorts of losses, grief, disasters, and catastrophes. Yet people worship and adore you. People fight, get arrested, and cheat each other, and I get blamed, even when it is not my fault. Sure, I'm evil, but give me a break. Can't you do something to make them stop blaming me?"

And so God created lawyers.

~♦~

A man sat down at a bar, looked into his shirt pocket, and ordered a double Scotch. A few minutes later, the man again peeked into his pocket and ordered another double. This routine was followed for some time, until after looking into his pocket, he told the bartender that he'd had enough.

The bartender said, "I've got to ask you—what's with the pocket business?"

The man replied, "I have my lawyer's picture in there. When he starts to look honest, I've had enough."

~✦~

An investment counselor went out on her own. She was shrewd and diligent, so business kept coming in, and pretty soon she realized she needed an in-house counsel, so she began interviewing young lawyers.

"As I'm sure you can understand," she started off with one of the first applicants, "in a business like this, our personal integrity must be beyond question." She leaned forward. "Mr. Anderson, are you an honest lawyer?"

"Honest," replied the applicant. "Let me tell you something about honesty. Why, I'm so honest that my father lent me twenty-five thousand dollars for my education and I paid back every penny the minute I tried my very first case."

"Impressive… And what sort of case was that?"

The lawyer squirmed in his seat and stated, "My father sued me for the loan money."

~✦~

A man walked into the local Chamber of Commerce of a small town, obviously desperate. Seeing a man at the counter, the stranger asks, "Is there a criminal attorney in town?" To which the man behind the counter immediately quipped, "Yeah, but we can't prove it yet!"

~◆~

Jury: A collection of people banded together for the purpose of deciding which side has hired the better lawyer.

~◆~

Two lawyers were walking along negotiating a case. "Look," said one, "let's be honest with each other." "Okay, you first," replied the other. That was the end of the discussion.

~♦~

A millionaire informs his attorney, "I want a stipulation in my Will that my wife is to inherit everything, but only if she remarries within six months of my death." "Why such an odd stipulation?" asked the attorney. "Because I want someone to be sorry I died!" came the reply.

~♦~

I broke a mirror the other day. That's seven years bad luck, but my lawyer thinks he can get me five.

~♦~

A man walks into a bar with an alligator. "Do you serve lawyers in here?" the man inquires. "Sure do!" replied the bartender. "Great!" said the man. "I'll have a Coors Light, and how 'bout a lawyer for my 'gator."

~♦~

Two law students are spending their Friday night studying for their big Constitutional Law exam on Monday morning. They study from 6:00PM to 8:30PM, when they decide to take a break.

They walk down to the nearest bar and have a drink. While there, the two meet a group of girls who invite them to a party.

The law students figure they will have time over the weekend to study, so they go to the party with the girls. They stay up all night partying and sleep all day Saturday.

Before they have a chance to get back home to spend their Sunday studying, the girls invite them to another party. The girls make a convincing argument, and the two law students decide to go to the next party.

On Monday morning, their heads are pounding. They can't make it out of bed in time for the exam. They wake up Monday afternoon and hurry to the professor's office to beg for a makeup test.

They tell the professor they were on their way to class when their car got a flat tire. They plead their case and eventually, the professor agrees to give them a makeup exam. The two law students share a devious grin, knowing they had duped the Professor. The professor puts the two students in separate rooms and administers the makeup exam, which has only two questions:

1. Explain the significance of habeus corpus in contemporary US law. (Value - 5% points)

2. Which tire? (Value - 95% points)

~♦~

A mobster was on trial, facing a possible life sentence, but his lawyer bribed a juror to hold out for a lesser charge.

After hours of deliberation, the jury returned a verdict carrying a maximum of ten years in prison.

Afterward, the lawyer approached the juror. "You had me so worried! When the jury was out so long, I was afraid you couldn't pull it off."

"I was worried too!" answered the juror. "The others all wanted to acquit him!"

~+~

A plane full of New York lawyers was heading for their annual Las Vegas Convention when it was hijacked. The plane was forced to land at Chicago's O'Hare Airport, and the hijackers radioed to ground control with a huge list of demands.

When asked what would happen if their demands weren't met the hijacker spokesman stated, "If you don't do exactly as we say, we will release one lawyer every single hour."

~✦~

A man was on trial for selling drugs, and a neighbor was called as a witness at the trial. The defense attorney asked the neighbor, "Did you ever get any cocaine or other drugs from the defendant?"

"No, sir," answered the witness.

"Did you ever get any from his wife?"

"No, sir."

"Did you ever get any from his daughters?" asked the attorney.

"Uh, excuse me, sir," the witness said, "but we're still talking about drugs here, aren't we?"

~✦~

A man walking along the beach one day finds a bottle. He rubs it and, sure enough, out popped a genie. "I will grant you three wishes," said the genie. "But there is a catch."

"What's that?" the man asked.

The genie replied, "Every time you make a wish, every lawyer in the world will receive double the wish you were granted."

"No problem!" replied the elated man.

The man's first wish was for a Ferrari. POOF! A Ferrari appeared. "Now every lawyer in the world has two Ferraris," said the genie.

"Next wish?" asked the genie.

"One million dollars," replied the man. POOF! One million dollars appeared at his feet. "Now every lawyer in the world has TWO million dollars," said the genie.

"Well, that's okay, as long as I have my million," replied the man.

"What is your third and final wish?" the genie wanted to know.

The man thought long and hard about all the lawyers he'd known and finally said, "Well, you know, I've always wanted to donate a kidney!"

~✦~

The owners of a bar were so sure that their bartender was the strongest man in the world that they offered $1,000 to anyone who could beat him in one task.

The bartender squeezed a lemon until all the juice ran out. Anyone who could get a drop of juice out of it after the bartender was done would win the $1,000.

Many strong people tried and failed until one day a scrawny man wearing thick glasses and a polyester suit came into the bar. He said, "I'd like to try the bet."

After the laughter died down, the bartender grabbed a lemon and squeezed away. Then he handed the rind to the man who, to everyone's amazement, squeezed six drops into the glass.

Stunned, the bartender paid up, and then asked the man, "What do you do for a living? Are you a lumberjack? A weight lifter?"

"No," the man replied. "I'm an attorney with the IRS."

~+~

A lawyer on his deathbed called out to his wife.

She rushed in and said, "What is it, darling?"

He told her to run and get the Bible as fast as possible.

Being a religious woman, she thought this was a good idea. She ran and got it and prepared to read him his favorite verse or something of the sort.

He snatched it from her and began quickly scanning pages, his eyes darting right and left.

The wife became curious, and asked, "What are you doing, darling?"

"I'm looking for loopholes!" he shouted.

~ + ~

Two lawyers are in a bank, when, suddenly, two armed robbers burst in.

While one of the robbers takes the money from the tellers, the other lines the customers, including the lawyers, up against a wall, and proceeds to take their wallets, watches, and other valuables.

The first lawyer shoves something into the other one's hand.

"What is this?" the latter asks without looking.

"It's that $100 I owe you."

~♦~

A personal injury lawyer was on vacation in a small rural town. While walking through the streets, he spotted a car that had just been involved in an accident. As expected, a large crowd gathered.

Going by instinct, the attorney was eager to get to the injured, but he couldn't get near the car. Being very clever, he started shouting loudly, "Let me through! Let me through! I am the son of the victim."

The crowd made way for him. Lying in front of the car was a donkey.

~✦~

A defense attorney's cross-examination of a police officer during a felony trial:

Q. Officer, did you see my client fleeing the scene?

A. No sir, but I subsequently observed a person matching the description of the offender running several blocks away.

Q. Officer, who provided this description?

A. The officer who responded to the scene.

Q. A fellow officer provided the description of this so-called offender. Do you trust your fellow officers?

A. Yes sir, with my life.

Q. With your life? Let me ask you this then officer, do you have a locker room in the police station, a room where you change your clothes in preparation for your daily duties?

A. Yes sir, we do.

Q. And do you have a locker in that room?

A. Yes sir, I do.

Q. And do you have a lock on your locker?

A. Yes, sir.

Q. Now why is it, officer, if you trust your fellow officers with your life, that you find it necessary to lock your locker in a room you share with those same officers?

A. You see, sir, we share the building with a court complex, and sometimes lawyers have been known to walk through that room.

~✦~

A noted criminal defense lawyer was making his closing argument for his client accused of murder, although the body of the victim had never been found. The lawyer dramatically turned to the courtroom's clock and, pointing to it, announced, "Ladies and gentlemen of the jury, I have some astounding news. I have found the supposed victim of this murder to be alive! In just ten seconds, she will walk through the door of this courtroom."

A heavy quiet fell over the courtroom as everyone waited for the dramatic entry. But nothing happened.

The lawyer continued, "The mere fact that you were watching the door, expecting the victim to walk into this courtroom, is clear proof that you have far more than even a reasonable doubt as to whether a murder was actually committed."

Smugly smiling at his cleverness, the lawyer confidently sat down to await acquittal, but the jury returned a guilty verdict in only ten minutes.

After the trial had ended, the dismayed lawyer asked the jury foreman: "Guilty? How could you convict? You were all watching the door!"

"Well," the foreman explained, "Most of us were watching the door. But one of us was watching the defendant, and he wasn't watching the door."

~✦~

A man is at his lawyer's funeral and is surprised by the turnout for this one man. He turns to the people around him. "Why are you all at this man's funeral?"

A man turns towards him and says, "We're all clients."

"And you *all* came to pay your respects? How touching."

"No, we came to make sure he was dead."

~+~

A man chosen for jury duty really wanted to be dismissed from serving. He tried every excuse he could think of but none of them worked. On the day of the trial, he decided to give it one more shot. As the trial was about to begin, he asked if he could approach the bench.

"Your Honor," he said, "I must be excused from this trial because I am prejudiced against the defendant. I took one look at the man in the blue suit with those beady eyes and that dishonest face and I said 'He's a crook! He's guilty!' So, Your Honor, I cannot possibly serve on this jury."

To which the judge replied, "Get back in the jury box, you fool. That man is the defendant's lawyer."

~+~

A stingy old lawyer who had been diagnosed with a terminal illness was determined to prove wrong the saying, "You can't take it with you."

After much thought and consideration, the old ambulance-chaser finally figured out how to take at least some of his money with him when he died. He instructed his wife to go to the bank and withdraw enough money to fill two pillow cases. He then directed her to take the bags of money to the attic and leave them directly above his bed. His plan: When he passed away, he would reach out and grab the bags on his way to heaven.

Several weeks after the funeral, his widow was up in the attic cleaning, and came upon the two forgotten pillow cases stuffed with cash. "Oh, that darn fool," she exclaimed, "I knew he should have had me put the money in the basement."

~✦~

A police chief, a fire chief, and a city attorney were traveling together to an out-of-state municipal management conference when their car broke down in a rural area, and they were forced to seek shelter for the night at a farmhouse. The farmer welcomed them but said that there were only two spare beds, and that one of the three would have to sleep in the barn with the farm animals.

The police chief agreed to take the barn. Shortly after the farmer and his guests went to bed, a knock was heard on the door of the farmhouse. The farmer opened the door and saw the police chief standing there, complaining that he could not sleep. There were pigs in the barn, he said, and he was reminded of the days when everyone called him a pig.

The fire chief then volunteered, but a short time later, another knock was heard. The fire chief complained that the cows in the barn reminded him of Mrs. O'Leary's cow that started the Chicago fire, and that every time he started to go to sleep, he began to have a nightmare about burning to death.

That left the city attorney, who trudged out to the barn. A few minutes later, another knock was heard. When the farmer answered the door, there stood some very indignant cows and pigs.

~♦~

A lawyer rolls through a stop sign and gets pulled over by a sheriff's deputy.

The deputy says, "license and registration, please."

"Why?" asks the lawyer.

The deputy says, "You didn't come to a complete stop at the stop sign."

The lawyer says, "I slowed down, and no one was coming."

"You still didn't come to a complete stop," says the deputy. "Your license and registration, please."

The lawyer says, "What's the difference?"

"The difference is you have to come to a complete stop, that's the law. License and registration, please."

The lawyer says, "If you can show me the legal difference between slow down and stop, I'll give you my license and registration and you give me the ticket. If not, you let me go and don't give me the ticket."

"That sounds fair. Please exit your vehicle, sir," the deputy says. The deputy then takes out his nightstick, starts beating the lawyer with it, and asks, "Do you want me to stop, or just slow down?"

~✦~

A lawyer purchased a box of very expensive cigars, then insured them against fire among other things. Within a month, having smoked his entire stockpile of these great cigars and without yet having made even his first premium payment on the policy, the lawyer filed a claim with the insurance company stating that the cigars were lost "in a series of small fires."

The insurance company refused to pay, citing the obvious reason: that the man had consumed the cigars in the normal fashion.

The lawyer sued . . . and won! The judge agreed with the insurance company that the claim was frivolous, but nevertheless, he held that the lawyer held a policy from the company in which it had warranted that the cigars were insurable and also guaranteed that it would insure them against fire, without defining what is considered to be "unacceptable fire," and was obligated to pay the claim.

Rather than endure a lengthy and costly appeal process, the insurance company accepted the ruling and paid $15,000 to the lawyer for his expensive cigars lost in the "fires."

However, after the lawyer cashed the check, the insurance company had him arrested on twenty-four counts of arson. With his own insurance claim and testimony from the previous case used against him, the lawyer was convicted of intentionally burning his insured property and was sentenced to 24 months in jail and a $24,000 fine.

~✦~

If an apple a day keeps the doctor away, how many orchards does it take to keep a lawyer away?

~♦~

Two physicians boarded a flight out of Seattle. One sat in the window seat, the other sat in the middle seat. Just before takeoff, an attorney got on and took the aisle seat next to the two physicians. The attorney kicked off his shoes, wiggled his toes, and was settling in when the physician in the window seat said, "I think I'll get up and get a Coke."

"No problem," said the attorney, "I'll get it for you."

While he was gone, one of the physicians picked up the attorney's shoe and put a thumbtack in it. When he returned with the soft drink, the other physician said, "That looks good, I think I'll have one too."

Again, the attorney obligingly went to fetch it and while he was gone, the other physician picked up the other shoe and put a tack in it. The attorney returned and they all sat back and enjoyed the flight.

As the plane was landing, the attorney slipped his feet into his shoes and knew immediately what had happened. "How long must this go on?" he asked. "This fighting between our professions? This hatred? This animosity? This putting tacks in shoes and spitting in Cokes?"

~♦~

A defendant in a lawsuit involving a very large sum of money said to his lawyer, "If I lose this case, I'll be ruined!"

"It's in the judge's hands now," said the lawyer.

"Would it help if I sent the judge a box of cigars?" asked the defendant.

"No!!! The judge is a stickler on ethical behavior. A stunt like that would prejudice him against you. He might even hold you in contempt of court."

A few weeks later, the judge rendered a decision in favor of the defendant. As the defendant left the courthouse, he said to his lawyer, "Thanks for the tip about the cigars. It really worked!"

Confidently the lawyer responded, "I'm sure we would have lost the case if you'd sent them."

"But I did send them," replied the man. "I just enclosed the plaintiff's business card."

~✦~

A doctor, a lawyer, a young boy, and a priest were out for a Sunday afternoon flight in a small private plane. Suddenly, the plane developed engine trouble, and in spite of the pilot's best efforts, the plane started to go down. The pilot grabbed a parachute, yelled to the passengers that they had better jump, and then bailed out. Unfortunately, only three parachutes remained.

The doctor grabbed one and said, "I'm a doctor, I save lives, so I must live," and bailed out.

The lawyer said, "I'm a lawyer and lawyers are the smartest people in the world. I deserve to live." He also grabbed a parachute and jumped.

The priest looked at the little boy and said, "My son, I've lived a long and full life. You are young and have your whole life ahead of you. Take the last parachute and live in peace."

The little boy handed the parachute back to the priest and said, "Not to worry, Father. The 'smartest man in the world' just took off with my backpack."

~+~

A defense lawyer in a case involving a traffic accident was putting the witnesses through an exacting cross-examination, and was taking great delight in getting witnesses to admit that they did not remember every single detail of the accident. The attorney knew that no witness has a perfect memory, and he had honed his skills in exploiting minor inconsistencies and lapses of memory.

"Did you actually see the accident?" he asked the next witness.

"Yes, sir."

"How far away were you when the accident happened?"

"I was thirty-four feet, seven and three-quarter inches away from the point of collision," replied the witness.

"Thirty-four feet, seven and three-quarter inches?" the attorney asked sarcastically. "Do you honestly expect us to believe that your memory is so good, and your sense of distance is so precise, that months after the accident you can come into court and give that type of detail?"

The witness replied calmly, "Sir, I had a hunch that some obnoxious, know-it-all lawyer would ask me the distance, and would try to make it seem like I was lying if I could not give an exact answer. So I got a tape measure and measured out the exact distance."

~+~

A fairly young big-time New York lawyer went duck hunting in rural Georgia. He shot a duck, but it fell into a farmer's field on the other side of the fence. As the lawyer started to climb over the fence to collect the bird, an elderly farmer drove up on his tractor and asked him what he was doing.

The lawyer replied, "I shot a duck and it fell in this field. Now I'm going in to retrieve it."

The old farmer looked the lawyer in the eyes and stated firmly, "This is my property, and you are not coming over here."

The lawyer huffed angrily, "I am one of the most famous trial lawyers in the country. If you don't let me get my duck, I'll sue you."

The old farmer smiled. "Apparently, you don't know how we do things in Gorgia.. We settle small disagreements like this with the Three Hit Rule."

The lawyer asked, "What's that?"

The farmer answered, "Well, first I kick you three times and then you kick me three times, and so on, back and forth, until someone gives up."

The attorney thought about the proposed contest and decided that he could easily take the old codger.

The old farmer slowly climbed down from the tractor and walked up to the lawyer. His first hit to the shin had the lawyer hopping around on one foot when suddenly the farmer planted the toe of his heavy work boot into the lawyer's groin and dropped him to his knees. The attorney was flat on his belly when the farmer's third kick to a kidney nearly caused him to pass out.

The lawyer summoned every bit of his will power and managed to get to his feet and said, "Okay, old man, now it's my turn."

The old farmer smiled and said, "Naw, I give up. You win, you can have the duck.

~+~

A farmer tells a lawyer he wants a divorce.

The attorney asks, "Well do you have any grounds?" The farmer said, "Yeah, I got me about 140 acres."

The attorney says, "No, you don't understand. Do you have a case?" The farmer says, "No, I don't have a Case, I have a John Deere."

The attorney says, "No, you don't understand. I mean do you have a grudge?" The farmer says, "Yeah, I got me a grudge, that's where I parks me John Deere."

The attorney says, "No sir, I mean do you have a suit?" The farmer says, "Yes sir, I got me a suit. I wear it to church on Sundays."

The exasperated attorney says, "Well sir, does your wife beat you up or anything?" The farmer says, "Oh no sir. We both get up about the same time, around 4:30."

Finally, the attorney says, "Okay, let me put it to you this way. "Why do you want a divorce from your wife?"

The farmer replied, "Well, I can never have me a meaningful conversation with her."

~+~

Ted was doing very well in his business and decided to reward himself with a long, luxurious stay at a very exclusive Caribbean resort. While relaxing on the beach, he was surprised to see a former high school classmate whom he hadn't seen since they graduated. His old friend had been something of a flake in high school, and this was the last place Ted expected to see him.

Ted approached the man, and seized his hand. "Jim, it's Ted from high school. It's sure been a long time. You look great! You must really be doing okay for yourself."

"I am," whispered Jim. "I am a partner with a large very successful law firm. But don't tell my mom. She got the idea that I was a drug dealer back when I was in high school, and she would be terribly disappointed if she figured out how I really make my money."

~✦~

Ms. Smith, a second grade teacher, asked her students what their parents did for a living. "Billy, you'll be first," she said. "What do your parents do?"

Billy stood up and proudly said, "My father is a professor and my mother is a doctor."

"That's wonderful," the teacher said, "and how about you, Teresa?"

Teresa shyly stood up, shuffled her feet and said, "My father is a mailman."

"What about your parents, Johnny?"

Johnny proudly stood up and announced, "My mother stays home to take care of us and my father plays piano in a whorehouse."

The teacher, stunned, promptly changed the subject to spelling. Later that day she called Johnny's house. Johnny's father answered the phone. The teacher explained what his son had said, and asked why he would say such a horrible thing.

Johnny's father explained, "I'm actually an attorney. But how can I explain a thing like that to a seven-year-old?"

~✦~

A lawyer was so large that when he died, the undertaker couldn't find a coffin big enough to hold the body.

So the undertaker gave him an enema and buried him in a shoebox.

~♦~

A man received a call from his attorney, insisting that they meet at once. He arrived at his attorney's office, and was ushered in immediately.

"Do you want the bad news first or the terrible news?" the attorney asked.

"Well, if those are my choices, I guess I'll take the bad news first."

"Your wife found a picture worth a half-million dollars."

"That's the bad news?" Bill was stunned. "If you call that bad, I can't wait to hear the terrible news."

"The terrible news is that the picture is of you and your mistress."

~♦~

A man woke up in a hospital bed and called for his doctor. He asked, "Give it to me straight. How long have I got?"

When the doctor said that he doubted that his patient would survive the night, the man said, "Call for my lawyer."

When the lawyer arrived, the patient asked him to stand on one side of the bed, while the doctor stood on the other. The patient then lay back and closed his eyes. When he remained silent for several minutes, the doctor inquired about what he was doing.

The patient replied, "Jesus died with a thief on either side, and I thought I'd check out the same way."

~✦~

A motorist who was caught in a speed trap in a small southern town was hauled before the local Justice of the Peace. The Justice fined the young man $200 and collected the money on the spot, but handed back the ticket.

"Just what am I supposed to do with this?" the motorist asked, "I paid my fine!" "Keep it," replied the Justice. "When you get three, you get a bicycle!"

~✦~

The lawyer's lawsuit-proof Christmas card:

Please accept without obligation, express or implied, these best wishes for an environmentally safe, socially responsible, low-stress, non-addictive, and gender-neutral celebration of the winter solstice holiday as practiced within the most enjoyable traditions of the religious persuasion of your choice (but with respect for the religious or secular persuasions and/or traditions of others, or for their choice not to practice religious or secular traditions at all) and further for a fiscally successful, personally fulfilling, and medically uncomplicated onset of the generally accepted calendar year (including, but not limited to, the Christian calendar, but not without due respect for the calendars of choice of other cultures). The preceding wishes are extended without regard to the race, creed, color, age, physical ability, religious faith, choice of computer platform, or sexual preference of the wishee(s).

~✦~

A banker and a lawyer got into a car accident on a small country road. The lawyer had figured that nobody else would be on the road, and had raced through a stop sign. The banker, on a cross street, had no time to react and couldn't have missed the lawyer if he had tried. Fortunately, neither driver was hurt.

The lawyer, seeing that the banker was a little shaken up, helped him from his battered car and offered him a drink from a hip flask. The banker accepted, took a deep drink, and handed the flask back to the lawyer. The lawyer held the flask for a minute or two, and gave it to the banker again. The banker took another swig. He again returned the flask to the lawyer, who closed it and put it away.

"Aren't you going to have a drink yourself?" asked the banker.

"Not now," answered the lawyer. "I'll have something after the police leave."

~+~

A Mexican bandit made a specialty of crossing the Rio Grande from time to time, robbing banks in Texas. Finally, a reward was offered for his capture, DEAD or ALIVE!

A trigger-happy, young, enterprising Texas Ranger decided to track down the bandit on his own and collect the reward. After a lengthy search, the Ranger tracked the bandit to his favorite cantina and snuck up behind him.

At the sound of the Ranger's guns cocking and preparing to fire, the surprised bandit turned around only to see both of the Ranger's six-shooters bearing down on him.

The Ranger announced, "You're under arrest! Tell me where you hid the loot or I'll drop you where you stand," his finger becoming itchy on the trigger.

However, the bandit didn't speak English and the Ranger didn't speak Spanish.

Fortunately for the Ranger, a bilingual lawyer was present in the cantina and translated the Ranger's demands to the bandit.

The terrified bandit blurted out, in Spanish, that the loot was buried next to an old oak tree behind the cantina.

"What did he say, what did he say?" the Ranger hurriedly asked.

To which the lawyer replied, "Well, the best I can make out he said . . . DRAW!"

~✦~

On their way to get married, a young couple was involved in a fatal car accident. They soon found themselves sitting outside the Pearly Gates waiting for St. Peter to process them into heaven. While waiting they began to wonder whether they might be married in heaven, and when Saint Peter arrived, they asked him.

Saint Peter said, "I don't know. This is the first time anyone has asked. Let me go find out," and he left.

The couple sat and waited—for two months—and as they waited, they discussed the pros and cons. If they were allowed to get married in heaven, should they get married, what with the eternal aspect of it all? "What if it doesn't work? Are we stuck in heaven together forever?"

Another month passed before Saint Peter finally returned, looking somewhat bedraggled. "Yes," he informed the couple, "You can get married in heaven."

"Great!" said the couple. "But we were just wondering; what if things don't work out? Could we also get a divorce in heaven?"

Red-faced with anger, Saint Peter stamped the ground. "What's wrong?" asked the frightened couple.

"Come on," Saint Peter shouted. "It took me three whole months to find a priest up here. Do you have any idea how long it'll take to find a lawyer?"

~❖~

A man is defending himself at trial after having been caught by a game warden just as he shot a spotted owl.

After reading the charges, the judge, well known for his environmental sympathies, gravely announced that since the species concerned is in danger of imminent extinction, he would have to make an example out of the defendant.

The man, waxing eloquent, said he was very sorry for what he'd done, but that he was totally destitute and needed the bird to feed his hungry children. All he had to his name, he said, his voice cracking with emotion, was the little bit of bird shot he had left in his gun.

The judge took off his glasses to wipe a tear from the corner of his eye, and after regaining his composure, told the defendant he would let him go with a warning this time.

As the hunter was leaving the courtroom, the judge called out, "Oh, by the way, what does a Spotted Owl taste like?"

"Your honor, it's hard to describe. Sort of a cross between a bald eagle, a whooping crane, and a California condor."

~✦~

A man was charged with stealing a car, and after a long trial, the jury acquitted him. Later that day the man came back to the judge who had presided at the hearing. "Your honor," he said, "I want to swear out a warrant for that lawyer of mine."

"Why?" asked the judge, "He won your acquittal. Why do you want to have him arrested?"

"Well, your honor," replied the man, "I didn't have the money to pay his fee, so he went and took the car I stole."

~✦~

Prosecutor: What were you doing on July 15 at 9 o'clock in the evening?

Prisoner: I was eating hamburger.

Prosecutor: What were you doing at 9:30 PM?

Prisoner: I was taking a bicarbonate of soda.

Prosecutor: Do you expect us to believe you?

Prisoner: You would if you had eaten one of those hamburgers.

~♦~

"You seem to have more than the average share of intelligence for a man of your background," sneered the lawyer at a witness on the stand.

"If I wasn't under oath, I'd return the compliment," replied the witness.

~+~

A man has a heart attack and is brought to the hospital ER. The doctor tells him that he will not live unless he has a heart transplant right away.

Another doctor runs into the room and says, "You're in luck, two hearts just became available, so you will get to choose which one you want. One belongs to an attorney and the other to a social worker."

The patient quickly responds, "the attorney's."

The doctor says, "Wait! Don't you want to know a little about them before you make your decision?"

The patient says, "I already know enough. We all know that social workers are bleeding hearts and the attorney probably never used his. So I'll take the attorney's!"

~+~

A doctor and a lawyer were talking at a party. Their conversation was constantly interrupted by people describing their ailments and asking the doctor for free medical advice. After an hour of this, the exasperated doctor asked the lawyer, "What do you do to stop people from asking you for legal advice when you're out of the office?"

"I give it to them," replied the lawyer, "and then I send them a bill."

The doctor was shocked, but agreed to give it a try.

The next day, still feeling slightly guilty, the doctor prepared the bills. When he went to place them in his mailbox, he found a bill from the lawyer.

~✦~

A lawyer defending a man accused of burglary tried this defense: "My client merely inserted his arm into the window and removed a few trifling articles. His arm is not himself, and I fail to see how you can punish the whole individual for an offense committed by his limb."

"Well put," the judge replied. "Using your logic, I sentence the defendant's arm to one year's imprisonment. He can accompany it or not, as he chooses."

The defendant smiled. With his lawyer's assistance he detached his artificial limb, laid it on the bench, and walked out.

~✦~

Following a distinguished legal career, a man arrived at the Gates of Heaven, accompanied by the Pope, who had the misfortune to expire on the same day. The Pope was greeted first by St. Peter, who escorted him to his quarters. The room was somewhat shabby and small, similar to that found in a low grade Motel-type establishment.

The lawyer was then taken to his room, which was a palatial suite including a private swimming pool, a garden, and a terrace overlooking the Gates. The attorney was somewhat taken aback, and told St. Peter, "I'm really quite surprised at these rooms, seeing as how the Pope was given such small accommodations."

St. Peter replied, "We have over a hundred Popes here but we've never had a lawyer before."

~✦~

A law firm receptionist answered the phone the morning after the firm's senior partner had passed away unexpectedly. "Is Mr. Spenser there?" asked the client on the phone.

"I'm very sorry, but Mr. Spenser passed away last night," the receptionist answered. "Can anyone else help you?"

The man paused for a moment, then quietly said, "no" and hung up.

Ten minutes later, he called again and asked for Mr. Spenser, his ex-wife's lawyer. The receptionist said, "You just called a few minutes ago, didn't you? Mr. Spenser has died. I'm not making this up." The man again hung up.

Fifteen minutes later, he called a third time and asked for Mr. Spenser. The receptionist was irked by this time. "I've told you twice already, Mr. Spenser is dead. He is not here! Why do you keep asking for him when I say he's dead? Don't you understand what I'm saying?"

The man replied, "I understand you perfectly. I just like hearing you say it over and over."

~✦~

A doctor, an architect, and an attorney were dining at the country club one day, and the conversation turned to the subject of their respective dogs, which were apparently quite extraordinary. A wager was placed on who had the most intelligent dog.

The physician offered to show his dog first, and called to the parking lot, "Hippocrates, come!" Hippocrates ran in, and was told by the doctor to do his stuff.

Hippocrates ran to the golf course and dug for a while, producing a number of bones. He dragged the bones into the country club, and assembled them into a complete, fully articulated human skeleton. The physician patted Hippocrates on the head, and gave him a cookie for his efforts.

The architect was only marginally impressed, and called for his dog, "Sliderule, come!" Sliderule ran in, and was told to do his stuff.

The dog immediately chewed the skeleton to rubble, but reassembled the fragments into a scale model of the Taj Mahal. The architect patted his dog and gave him a cookie.

The attorney watched the other two dogs, and called "Tort-Feasor, come!" The dog entered and was told to do his stuff.

Tort-Feasor immediately attacked the other two dogs, stole their cookies, auctioned the Taj Mahal replica to the other club members for his fee, and went outside to play golf.

~✦~

A trial had been scheduled in a small town, but the court clerk had forgotten to summon a jury pool. Rather than adjourning what he thought was an exceptionally simple case, the judge ordered his bailiff to go through the courthouse and round up enough people to form a jury. The bailiff returned with a group of lawyers.

The prosecutor felt that it would be an interesting experiment to try a case before a jury of lawyers, and the defense counsel had no objection, so a jury was impaneled. The trial went very quickly—after only an hour of testimony, and very short closing arguments, both sides rested. The jury was then instructed by the judge, and sent back to the jury room to deliberate.

After nearly six hours, the trial court was concerned that the jury had not returned with a verdict. The case had in fact turned out to be every bit as simple as he had expected, and it seemed to him that they should have been back in minutes. He sent the bailiff to the jury room, to see if they needed anything.

The bailiff returned, and the judge asked, "Are they close to reaching a verdict?" The bailiff shook his head. "Your Honor, they're still doing nomination speeches for the position of foreman."

~ ✦ ~

There was an engineer who was tragically hit by a bus and killed instantly. He had lead a good life, but for some reason he found himself, rather than at the pearly gates, in the "Other Place." Not one to complain, he shrugged and submitted himself to the tortures and other indignities common in Hell.

Soon after he arrived, there was a problem with one of the many furnaces. The engineer was happy to help out (he volunteered as he wanted a challenge) and before long it was up and running again.

This brought him to the attention of one of the senior demons that then had him working all over Hell fixing the torture devices, working out the kinks in the plumbing system, installing digital controls to the flame throwers . . . you name it.

Pretty soon word reached Satan that Hell had a great new addition to the team. The engineer was then asked to plan and oversee the creation of a giant new computer network.

Word of all these improvements reached Heaven. God was upset and had St. Peter look into the details. Then God called Satan and told him he wanted the engineer back.

"Nothing doing," said Satan, "You sent him down here, and we're keeping him!"

"What?" sputtered God, "You get him up here right now! That's a direct order!"

"Listen pal, I don't take orders from you any more. Remember that 'rule in hell' agreement?"

God was beside himself. "If you don't send that engineer up here right now, I'll . . . I'll sue you!"

"Oh, sure!" Satan shot back gleefully. "Where are you going to get a lawyer?"

~+~

After meeting with an elderly lady to draft her will, the attorney charged her $100.

She gave him a $100 bill, not noticing that it was stuck to another $100 bill.

On seeing the two bills stuck together, the ethical question came to the attorney's mind: "Do I tell my partner?"

~+~

When a person assists a criminal in breaking the law before the criminal gets arrested, we call him an accomplice.

When a person assists a criminal in breaking the law after the criminal gets arrested, we call him a defense lawyer.

~✦~

Taylor was desperate for business, and was happy to be appointed by the court to defend an indigent defendant. The judge ordered Taylor, "You are to confer with the defendant in the hallway, and give him the best legal advice you can."

After a time, Taylor re-entered the courtroom alone.

When the judge asked where the defendant had gone, Taylor replied, "You asked me to give him good advice. I found out that he was guilty, so I told him to run like hell."

~✦~

A lawyer had a summer house in the wilds of Maine to which he retreated for several weeks of the year. Each summer, the lawyer would invite a different friend to spend a week or two there.

On one particular occasion, he invited a Czechoslovakian friend to stay with him. The friend, eager to get a freebie off a lawyer, agreed. Well, they had a splendid time in the country, rising early and living in the great outdoors.

Early one morning, the lawyer and his friend went out to pick berries for their morning breakfast. As they went around the berry patch, gathering blueberries and raspberries in tremendous quantities, along came two huge bears, a male and a female. The lawyer, seeing the two bears, immediately dashed for cover. His friend, though, wasn't so lucky, and the male bear reached him and swallowed him whole.

The lawyer ran back to his Mercedes, tore into town as fast as he could, and got the local backwoods sheriff. The sheriff grabbed his shotgun and dashed back to the berry patch with the lawyer. Sure enough, the two bears were still there.

"He's in that one!" cried the lawyer, pointing to the male, while visions of lawsuits from his friend's family danced in his head.

He just had to save his friend. The sheriff looked at the bears, and without batting an eye, leveled his gun, took careful aim, and shot the female.

"Whatdya do that for!" exclaimed the lawyer, "I said he was in the other!"

"Exactly," replied the sheriff, "and would you believe a lawyer who told you that the Czech was in the male?"

~❖~

Two New York City law partners hired a secretary from a small Midwestern town. She was attractive, but it was obvious that she knew nothing about city life.

One attorney said to the other, "Mary is so young and pretty she might be taken advantage of by fast-talking city guys. Why don't we teach her what's right and what's wrong?"

"Great idea," said the partner. "You teach her what's right."

~ ✦ ~

A man noticed that his neighbor's car was covered with leaves, grass, branches, dirt, and blood. "What in the world happened to your car?"

"I ran into a lawyer," said the neighbor.

"Well," said the man, "that explains the blood. But what about the leaves, the grass, the branches, and all of the dirt?"

His neighbor replied, "I had to chase him all through the park."

~♦~

Bill and Ernie, two second-story men from Los Angeles, were comparing notes on recent burglaries.

"Did you get anything on that last heist?" Bill asked.

"Nothing at all," Ernie admitted. "Turns out that the guy that lives there's a lawyer."

"Jeez, aren't those the breaks," his friend sympathized. "Did you lose anything?"

~♦~

One day at a trial, an eminent psychologist was called to testify. A severe, no-nonsense professional, she sat down in the witness chair, unaware that its rear legs were set precariously on the back of the raised platform.

"Will you state your name?" asked the district attorney. Tilting back in her chair she opened her mouth to answer, but instead catapulted head-over-heels backward and landed in a stack of exhibits and recording equipment.

"Well, doctor," continued the district attorney without changing expression, "we could start with an easier question".

~ + ~

Mrs. Smith, the 5th grade teacher, posed the following problem to one of her classes: "A wealthy man dies and leaves 100 million dollars. One-fifth is to go to his wife, one-fifth is to go to his son, one-sixth to his butler, and the rest to charity. Now, what does each get?"

After a very long silence in the classroom, little Timmy raised his hand and answered, "A lawyer!"

~♦~

After his graduation from college, the son of a lawyer was considering his future. He went to his father and asked if he might be given a desk in the corner from which he could observe his father's activities and be introduced to his father's clients as a clerk. His observations would help him decide whether or not to go to law school to become a lawyer. His father thought this was a great idea and immediately helped to set it up.

The first client the next morning was a tenant farmer, a rough man with calloused hands who was dressed in workman's clothing.

He said, "Mr. Lawyer, I work for the Henderson farm on the east side of town. For many years I have tended their crops and animals, including some cows. I have raised the cows, fed them and looked after them. And I was always given the understanding and the belief that I was the owner of these cows. Now Mr. Henderson has died and his son has inherited the farm. He believes that since the cows were raised on his land and ate his hay, the cows are his. In short, we are in dispute over who owns the cows."

The lawyer said, "Thank you. I have heard enough. I will take your case. Don't worry about the cows!"

The next client to come in, a well-dressed young man, was obviously a landowner. He said, "My name is Henderson and I own a farm on the east side of town. We have a tenant farmer who has worked for my family for many years, tending crops and the animals, including some cows. I believe the cows belong to me because they were raised on my land and were fed my hay. But the tenant farmer believes they are his because he raised them and cared for them. In short, we are in dispute over who owns the cows."

The lawyer said, "Thank you. I have heard enough. I will take your case. Don't worry about the cows!"

After the client left, the lawyer's son could not help but express his concern. "Father, I know very little about the law, but it seems we have a very serious problem concerning these cows."

"Don't worry about the cows!" the lawyer said. "The cows will be ours!"

~✦~

One day in Contract Law class, Professor Jepson asked one of his better students, "Now if you were to give someone an orange, how would you go about it?"

The student replied, "Here's an orange."

The professor was livid. "No! No! Think like a lawyer!"

The student then recited, "Okay, I'd tell him, 'I hereby give and convey to you all and singular, my estate and interests, rights, claim, title, calim and advantages of and in, said orange, together with all its rind, juice, pulp, and seeds, and all rights and advantages with full power to bite, cut, freeze, and otherwise eat, the same, or give the same away with and without the pulp, juice, rind, and seeds, anything herein before or hereinafter or in any deed, or deeds, instruments of whatever nature or kind whatsoever to the contrary in anywise notwithstanding..."

~✦~

A lawyer was briefing his client, who was about to testify in his own defense.

"You must swear to tell the complete truth. Do you understand?"

The client replied that he did.

The lawyer then asked, "Do you know what will happen if you don't tell the truth?"

The client looked back and said, "I imagine that our side will win."

~✦~

A junior partner in a law firm was sent to the state capital to represent a long-term client accused of robbery. After days of trial, the case was won, the client acquitted and released.

Excited about his success, the attorney e-mailed the firm: "Justice prevailed."

The senior partner sent his reply one second later, "Appeal immediately."

~✦~

An engineer, a physicist, and a lawyer were being interviewed for a position as chief executive officer of a large corporation. The engineer was interviewed first, and was asked a long list of questions, ending with "How much is two plus two?" The engineer excused himself, and made a series of measurements and calculations before returning to the board room and announcing, "Four."

The physicist was next interviewed, and was asked the same questions. Again, the last question was, "How much is two plus two?" Before answering the last question, he excused himself, made for the library, and did a great deal of research. After a consultation with the United States Bureau of Standards and many calculations, he also announced, "Four."

The lawyer was interviewed last, and again the final question was, "How much is two plus two?" The lawyer drew all the shades in the room, looked outside to see if anyone was there, checked the telephone for listening devices, and then whispered, "How much do you want it to be?"

~+~

A lawyer was filling out a job application when he came to the question: "Have you ever been arrested?"

He answered "no."

The next question, intended for those who answered the preceding question with a yes, was "why?"

Nevertheless, the lawyer answered it "Never got caught."

~+~

A water pipe burst in a lawyer's office so he called a plumber. The plumber arrived, unpacked his tools, did mysterious plumber types of things for a while, and handed the lawyer a bill for $500.

The lawyer exclaimed, "This is ridiculous! I don't even make that much as a lawyer."

The plumber replied, "Neither did I when I was a lawyer."

~+~

A gang of robbers broke into a lawyer's club by mistake. The legal lions gave them a fight for their life and their money. The gang was very happy to escape.

"It ain't so bad," one crook noted. "We got $25 between us."

The boss screamed: "I warned you to stay clear of lawyers—we had $100 when we broke in!"

~✦~

An elderly and somewhat hard-of-hearing man was sitting in a stylish downtown attorney's office as his lawyer handed him his will. "Your estate is very complex," said the lawyer, "but I've made sure that all of your wishes will be executed. Due to the complexity, my fee is $4,500."

Just then, the phone rang and the lawyer got involved with a long call. Thinking the lawyer had said "$500," the old man wrote out his check and left.

When she got off the phone and realized the client's mistake, the lawyer ran after him down the stairs and into the parking lot just as he drove away. Feeling frustrated, the lawyer looked at the check and decided to accept the situation philosophically. "Oh well," she said to herself, "$500 for fifteen minutes' work isn't bad."

~✦~

St. Peter is questioning three married couples to see if they qualify for admittance to heaven. "Why do you deserve to pass the Pearly Gates?" he asks one of the men, who had been a butler.

"I was a good father," he answers.

"Yes, but you were a drunk all your life. In fact, you were so bad you even married a woman named Sherry. No admittance."

St. Peter then turned to the next man, a carpenter, and asked him the same question.

The carpenter replied that he had worked hard and taken good care of his family.

But St. Peter also rejected him, pointing out that he had been an impossible glutton, so much so that he married a woman named BonBon.

At this point the third man, who had been a lawyer, stood up and said, "Come on, Penny, let's get out of here."

~ ✦ ~

A lawyer was driving his big BMW down the highway, singing to himself, "I love my BMW, I love my BMW." Focusing on his car, not his driving, he smashed into a tree. He miraculously survived, but his car was totaled. "My BMW! My BMW!" he sobbed.

A good Samaritan drove by and cried out, "Sir, sir, you're bleeding! And my God, your left arm is gone!"

The lawyer looked down and screamed, "My Rolex! My Rolex!"

~✦~

A lawyer is cross-examining a doctor on the witness stand about whether or not he had checked the pulse of the deceased before he signed the death certificate.

"No," the doctor said, "I did not check his pulse."

"And did you listen for a heartbeat?" said the lawyer.

"No, I did not," said the doctor.

"So," said the lawyer, "when you signed the death certificate, you had not taken steps to make sure he was dead."

The doctor, having enough of the lawyer's ridicule, stated, "Well, let me put it this way. The man's brain was in a jar on my desk, but for all I know he could be out practicing law somewhere."

~♦~

A physician, an engineer, and a lawyer were arguing about whose profession was the oldest.

The surgeon said, "Remember how God removed a rib from Adam to create Eve? Obviously, medicine is the oldest profession."

The engineer replied, "But before that, God created the heavens and the earth from chaos, in less than a week. You have to admit that was a remarkable feat of engineering, and that makes engineering an older profession than medicine."

The lawyer smirked and asked, "And who do you think created the chaos?"

~♦~

NASA was interviewing professionals to be sent to Mars. One that would go and couldn't return to Earth.

The first applicant, an engineer, was asked how much he wanted to be paid for going. "A million dollars," he answered, "because I want to donate it to M.I.T."

The next applicant, a doctor, was asked the same question. He asked for $2 million. "I want to give a million to my family," he explained, "and leave the other million for the advancement of medical research."

The last applicant was a lawyer. When asked how much money he wanted, he whispered in the interviewer's ear, "Three million dollars."

"Why so much more than the others?" asked the interviewer.

The lawyer replied, "If you give me $3 million, I'll give you $1 million, I'll keep $1 million, and we'll send the engineer to Mars."

~✦~

Two women are on a transcontinental balloon voyage. Their craft is engulfed in fog, their compass gone awry. Afraid of landing in the ocean, they drift for days. Suddenly, the clouds part to show a sunlit meadow below. As they descend, they see a man walking his dog.

One of the flyers yells to the figure far below, "Where are we?"

The man yells back, "About a half mile from town."

Once again, the balloonists are engulfed in the mist. One flyer says to the other, "He must have been a lawyer."

The other says, "A lawyer! How do you know that?"

The first says, "That's easy. The information he gave us was accurate, concise, and entirely irrelevant."

~+~

Two squirrels were walking along in the forest. The first one spied a nut and cried out, "Oh, look. A nut!" The second squirrel jumped on it and said, "It's my nut!"

The first squirrel said, "That's not fair! I saw it first!"

"Well, you may have seen it, but I have it," argued the second.

At that point, a lawyer squirrel came up and said, "You shouldn't quarrel. Let me resolve this dispute." The two squirrels nodded, and the lawyer squirrel said, "Now, give me the nut." He broke the nut in half, and handed half to each squirrel, saying, "See. It was foolish of you to fight. Now the dispute is resolved."

Then he reached over and said, "And for my fee, I'll take the meat."

~＊~

A man who had been caught embezzling millions from his employer went to a lawyer seeking defense. He didn't want to go to jail. His lawyer told him, "Don't worry. You'll never have to go to jail with all that money."

And the lawyer was right. When the man was sent to prison, he didn't have a dime left.

~✦~

A volunteer at the United Way in a fairly small town noticed that the most successful lawyer in the whole town hadn't made a contribution. This guy was making about $600,000 a year so the volunteer thought, "Why not call him up?"

He began with "Sir, according to our research you haven't made a contribution to the United Way, would you like to do so?"

The lawyer responds, "A contribution? Does your research show that I have an invalid mother who requires expensive surgery once a year just to stay alive?"

The worker is feeling a bit embarrassed and says, "Well, no sir, I'm..."

"Does your research show that my sister's husband was killed in a car accident? She has three kids and no means of support!"

The worker is feeling quite embarrassed at this point. "I'm terribly sorry..."

"Does your research show that my brother broke his neck on the job and now requires a full time nurse to have any kind of normal life?"

The worker is completely humiliated at this point. "I am sorry sir, please forgive me..."

"The gall of you people!," the lawyer went on. "I don't give them anything, so why should I give it to you!"

~♦~

The day after a verdict had been entered against his client, the lawyer rushed to the judge's chambers, demanding that the case be reopened, saying: "I have new evidence that makes a huge difference in my client's defense."

The judge asked, "What new evidence could you have?"

The lawyer replied, "My client has an extra $10,000, and I just found out about it!"

~+~

An old man was on his death bed. He wanted badly to take some of his money with him. He called his priest, his doctor, and his lawyer to his bedside. "Here's $30,000 cash to be held by each of you. I trust you to put this in my coffin when I die so I can take all my money with me."

At the funeral, each man put an envelope in the coffin. Riding away in a limousine, the priest suddenly broke into tears and confessed, "I had only put $20,000 into the envelope because I needed $10,000 for a new baptistery."

"Well, since we're confiding in each other," said the doctor, "I only put $10,000 in the envelope because we needed a new machine at the hospital which cost $20,000."

The lawyer was aghast. "I'm ashamed of both of you," he exclaimed. "I want it known that when I put my envelope in that coffin, it held my personal check for the full $30,000."

~+~

Lawyer: Let me give you my honest opinion.
Client: No, thank you—I'm paying for professional advice.

~♦~

A lawyer died and arrived at the Pearly Gates. To his dismay, there were thousands of people ahead of him in line to see St. Peter. However, and to the lawyer's surprise, St. Peter left his desk at the gate and came down the long line to where the lawyer was standing. St. Peter greeted him warmly. Then St. Peter and one of his assistants took the lawyer by the hands and guided him up to the front of the line into a comfortable chair by his desk.

The lawyer said, "I don't mind all this attention, but what makes me so special?"

St. Peter replied, "Well, I've added up all the hours for which you billed your clients, and by my calculation you must be about 150 years old!"

~♦~

The devil visited a lawyer's office and made him an offer. "I can arrange some things for you," the devil said. "I'll increase your income five-fold. Your partners will love you; your clients will respect you; you'll have four months of vacation each year and live to be a hundred. All I require in return is that your wife's soul, your children's souls, and their children's souls rot in hell for eternity."

The lawyer thought for a moment, then asked, "What's the catch?"

~✦~

A paralegal, an associate, and a partner of a law firm are walking through a park on their way to lunch when they find an antique oil lamp. They rub it and a genie comes out in a puff of smoke. The genie says: "I usually only grant three wishes, so I'll give each of you just one each".

"Me first! Me first!" says the paralegal. "I want to be in the Bahamas, driving a speedboat, without a care in the world."

Poof! He's gone.

"Me next! Me next!" says the associate. "I want to be in Hawaii, relaxing on the beach with my personal masseuse, an endless supply of pina coladas, and the love of my life."

Poof! Off she goes too.

"You're next," the genie tells the partner.

The partner says, "I want those two back in the library after lunch."

~✦~

A barber gave a haircut to a priest one day. The priest tried to pay for the haircut but the barber refused, saying, "I cannot accept money from you, for you are a good man—you do God's work."

The next morning the barber found a dozen bibles at the door to his shop. A policeman came to the barber for a haircut, and again the barber refused payment saying, "I cannot accept money from you, for you are a good man—you protect the public." The next morning the barber found a dozen doughnuts at the door to his shop.

A lawyer came to the barber for a haircut, and again the barber refused payment saying, "I cannot accept money from you, for you are a good man—you serve the justice system."

The next morning the barber found a dozen more lawyers waiting for a haircut.

~✦~

Two alligators sat on the edge of a swamp. The small one turned to the big one and said, "I don't understand how you can be so much bigger than I am. We're the same age, we were the same size as kids . . . I just don't get it."

"Well," said the big alligator, "what have you been eating?"

"Lawyers, same as you," replied the small alligator.

"Hmm. Well, where do you catch 'em?"

"Down at that law firm on the edge of the swamp."

"Same here. Hmm. How do you catch 'em?"

"Well, I crawl under a BMW and wait for someone to unlock the door. Then I jump out, bite 'em, shake the crap out of 'em, and eat 'em!"

"Ah!" said the big alligator, "I think I see your problem. See, by the time you get done shakin' the crap out of a lawyer, there's nothing left but lips and a briefcase . . ."

~✦~

The Postal Service just had to recall their latest new stamp issue. Lawyers were part of the design and people couldn't figure out which side to spit on.

~ ♦ ~

One day a teacher, a garbage collector, and a lawyer all died and went to heaven.

Because heaven was getting crowded, when they got to the gate St. Peter informed them that there would be a test to get into Heaven; they each had to answer a single question.

To the teacher, he asked, "What was the name of the ship that crashed into an iceberg and sunk with all its passengers?"

The teacher thought for a second, and then replied: "The *Titanic*." St. Peter let him through the gate.

Next, St. Peter turned to the garbage man, and figuring that heaven didn't really need all the stink that this guy would bring in, decided to make the question a little harder. "How many people died on the ship?"

The garbage man guessed 1228, to which St. Peter said, "That happens to be right. Go ahead."

St. Peter then turned to the lawyer. "What were their names?"

~ ♦ ~

A guy walks into a post office one day to see a middle-aged, balding man standing at the counter methodically placing "Love" stamps on bright pink envelopes with hearts all over them. He then takes out a perfume bottle and starts spraying scent all over them.

His curiosity getting the better of him, he goes up to the balding man and asks him what he is doing. The man says, "I'm sending out 1,000 Valentine cards signed, 'Guess who?'"

"But why?" asks the man.

"I'm a divorce lawyer," the man replies.

~+~

A truck driver used to amuse himself by running over lawyers he saw walking down the side of the road. Every time he saw a lawyer walking along the road, he swerved to hit him and there would be a loud *thump*. Then he would swerve back on the road.

One day, as the truck driver was driving along the road he saw a priest hitchhiking. He thought he would do a good deed and pulled the truck over.

"Where are you going, Father?" The truck driver asked.

"I'm going to the church five miles down the road," replied the priest.

"No problem, Father! I'll give you a lift. Climb in the truck." The happy priest climbed into the passenger seat and the truck driver continued down the road. Suddenly, the truck driver saw a lawyer walking down the road.

Instinctively he swerved to hit him. At the last moment he remembered there was a priest in the truck with him, so he swerved back to the road and narrowly missed the lawyer.

Certain he should've missed the lawyer, the truck driver was very surprised and immediately uneasy when he heard a loud *thump*. He felt really guilty about his actions and so turned to the priest and said, "I'm really sorry Father. I almost hit that lawyer."

"That's okay," replied the priest. "I got him with the door."

~✦~

A group of dinner guests were blaming all of America's troubles on lawyers when a woman said, "They aren't all so bad. Why, last year a lawyer gave me $1,000."

"I don't believe it," the host responded.

"It's true, I swear it," said the woman. "I had a complicated personal injury case and what with the lawyer's fee, the cost of expert witnesses, the cost of the appeal and other expenses, my bill was $41,000. When the judgment only amounted to $40,000, my lawyer simply forgave the difference."

~♦~

A local newspaper mistakenly printed an obituary for the town's oldest practicing lawyer. He called them immediately and threatened to sue unless they printed a correction.

The next day, the following notice appeared, "We regret that the report of Attorney Critchley's death was in error."

~♦~

Having just moved to a new home, a young boy meets the boy next door. "Hi, my name is Billy," he says, "what's yours?"

"Tommy," replied the other.

"My daddy's an accountant," says Billy. "What does your daddy do?"

"He's a lawyer," Tommy answers.

"Honest?" says Billy.

"No, just the regular kind."

~✦~

Someone mistakenly left the cages open in the Reptile House at the zoo and there were snakes slithering all over the place.

Frantically, the keeper tried everything, but he couldn't get the slippery animals back into their cages. Finally, he yelled,

"Quick, call a lawyer!"

"A lawyer? Why?"

"We need someone who speaks their language."

~✦~

"How is it that you can't get a lawyer to defend you?" the judge asked the prisoner.

"Well, Your Honor, as soon as those lawyers found out I didn't steal the money, they wouldn't have anything to do with me."

~✦~

A blonde and a lawyer are seated next to each other on a flight from LA to NY. The lawyer asks if she would like to play a fun game. The blonde, very tired, just wants to take a nap, so she politely declines and rolls over toward the window to catch a few winks. The lawyer persists (as lawyers are wont to do) and explains that the game is easy and a lot of fun. He says, "I ask you a question, and if you don't know the answer, you pay me $5.00 and vice versa."

Again, she declines and tries to get some sleep.

The lawyer, now agitated, says, "Okay, if you don't know the answer you pay me $5.00, and if I don't know the answer, I'll pay you $500.00."

This catches the blonde's attention and, figuring there will be no end to the torment unless she plays, agrees to the game.

The lawyer asks the first question, "What's the distance from the earth to the moon?"

The blonde doesn't say a word, reaches in her purse, pulls out a $5 bill and hands it to the lawyer.

"Okay," says the lawyer, "your turn."

She asks the lawyer, "What goes up a hill with three legs and comes down with four legs?"

The lawyer, puzzled, takes out his laptop computer and searches all his references, no answer. He taps into the air phone with his modem and searches the Web and Library of Congress, but still no answer. Frustrated, he sends e-mails to all his friends and coworkers, all to no avail. After an hour, he wakes the blonde and hands her $500.

The blonde says, "Thank you," and turns back to get some more sleep.

The lawyer, more than a little miffed, wakes the blonde and asks, "Well, what's the answer?"

Without a word, the blonde reaches in her purse, hands the lawyer $5.00, and goes back to sleep.

~♦~

A guy asked a friend how he was so successful at picking up women.

The friend replied, "It's simple. I just say I'm a lawyer."

So the guy went to a bar and approached a pretty woman and asked her out. After she said no, he told her that it was probably a good thing because he had a case early in the morning.

She said, "Oh!!!! You're a lawyer?"

He said, "Why, yes I am!" so they went to his place and when they were in bed, screwing, he started to laugh to himself. When she asked what was so funny, he answered, "Well, I've only been a lawyer for 15 minutes, and I'm already screwing someone!"

~✦~

The National Institutes of Health announced it will no longer use rats for medical experimentation. In their place, the NIH will use lawyers.

The NIH gave three reasons for this decision:

1. There are now more attorneys than there are rats.

2. The medical researchers don't become as emotionally attached to the attorneys as they did to the rats.

3. No matter how hard you try, there are some things that rats won't do.

~+~

When a divorce lawyer died and arrived at the pearly gates, Saint Peter asked him, "What have you done to merit entrance into Heaven?"

The lawyer thought a moment, then said, "A week ago, I gave a quarter to a homeless person on the street."

Saint Peter asked Gabriel to check the record, and Gabriel affirmed that this was true. Saint Peter told the lawyer, "That's fine, but it's not really quite enough to get you into Heaven."

The lawyer replied, "Well, three years ago I also gave another homeless person a quarter."

Saint Peter nodded to Gabriel, and after the angel nodded back, Saint Peter then whispered , "Well, what do you suggest we do with this fellow?"

Gabriel glanced at the lawyer, then said to Saint Peter, "Let's give him back his 50 cents and tell him to go to Hell."

~✦~

I broke a mirror, which means I'll get seven years of bad luck. However, my lawyer thinks he can get me only five.

~+~

For three years, a young bachelor attorney had been taking his vacations at a country inn. The previous year he finally seduced the innkeeper's daughter. Looking forward to an exciting few days, he dragged his suitcase up the stairs of the inn, then stopped short. There sat the young woman with an infant on her lap! "She's yours," she told the lawyer.

"Helen, why didn't you write when you learned you were pregnant?" he cried. "I would have rushed up here, we could have gotten married, and the baby would have my name!"

"Well," she said, "when my folks found out about my condition, we sat up all night talkin' and talkin' . The upshot was we decided it would be better to have a bastard than a lawyer in the family."

~+~

A Frenchman, an Englishman, an American, and a lawyer were sitting on a train. The Frenchman offered everyone a loaf of French bread, then threw it out the window. "Not to worry," he said, "we have plenty of those where I come from."

The Englishman offered everyone a crumpet and then he threw them out the window, saying, "don't worry we have plenty of those where I come from."

The American threw the lawyer out the window, saying, "don't worry we have plenty of those where *I* come from."

~♦~

There's a sushi bar that caters exclusively to lawyers – it's called "Sosumi."

~✦~

Did you hear about the British lady barrister who dropped her briefs and became a solicitor?

~✦~

Lawyer: Now that you have been acquitted, will you tell me honestly—did you steal the car?'

Client: After hearing your summation in court this morning, I'm beginning to think I didn't.

~✦~

Have you seen the current remake of the movie *Cape Fear*? It's about a deranged psychotic who is seeking revenge against a lawyer. The question is, while watching the movie, for whom do you root?

~✦~

An airliner was having engine trouble, and the pilot instructed the cabin crew to have the passengers take their seats and get prepared for an emergency landing. A few minutes later, the pilot asked the flight attendants if everyone was buckled in and ready. "All set back here, Captain," came the reply, except the lawyers are still going around passing out business cards.

~✦~

A young lawyer, starting up his private practice, was very anxious to impress potential clients. When he saw the first visitor to his office come through the door, he immediately picked up his phone and spoke into it, "I'm sorry, but my caseload is so tremendous that I'm not going to be able to look into your problem for at least a month. I'll have to get back to you then." He then turned to the man who had just walked in and said, "Now, what can I do for you?" "Nothing," replied the man. "I'm here to hook up your phone."

~✦~

A reporter outside of a courtroom asked a defendant clad only in a barrel: 'Oh, I see your attorney lost the case!' The defendant answered, 'No, we won. '

~+~

A prominent lawyer's son dreamed of following in his father's footsteps. After graduating from college and law school with honors, he returned home to join his father's firm, intent on proving himself to be a skilled and worthy attorney. At the end of his first day at work he rushed into his father's office, and said, 'Father, father! The Smith case, that you always said would go on forever — the one you have been toiling on for ten years — in one single day, I settled that case and saved the client a fortune!' His father frowned, and scolded his son, 'I did not say that it would go on forever, son. I said that it could go on forever. When you saw me toiling on that case for days and weeks at a time, didn't it ever occur to you that I was billing by the hour?'

~+~

CHAPTER TWO

Asked and Answered

— HUMOR IN BRIEF

Q: What's wrong with lawyer jokes?

A: Lawyers don't think they're funny, and nobody else thinks they're jokes.

~ ✦ ~

Q: How many lawyer jokes are there?

A: Just two . . . all the rest are true.

~ ✦ ~

Q: What is a contingent fee?

A: A contingent fee means, if the lawyer doesn't win your case, he gets nothing. If the lawyer does win it, you get nothing.

~+~

Q: What's the difference between a bad lawyer and a good lawyer?

A: A bad lawyer can let a case drag out for several years. A good lawyer can make it last even longer.

~+~

Q: What can a goose do, a duck can't, and a lawyer should?
A: Stick his bill up his ass.

~+~

Q: What is the difference between a mosquito and a lawyer?

A: One is a blood-sucking parasite. The other is an insect.

~ * ~

Q: How can you tell when a lawyer is lying?

A: His lips are moving.

~ * ~

Q: How do you get a group of lawyers to smile for a picture?

A: Just say "Fees!"

~ * ~

Q: What do you call a lawyer with an I.Q. of under 60?
A: Senator.

~•~

Q: Why are there so many lawyers in America?
A: Because St. Patrick chased the snakes out of Ireland.

~•~

Q: What's the difference between a lawyer and a herd of buffalo?
A: The lawyer charges more.

~•~

Q: "I hear you lost your court case. Did your lawyer give you bad advice?"

A: "No. He charged me for it."

~♦~

Q: What's an example of a lucky break?

A: When a busload of lawyers goes off a cliff.

~♦~

Q: What's an example of a crying shame?

A: There was an empty seat on the bus.

~♦~

Q: What do you get when you cross The Godfather with a lawyer?

A: An offer you can't understand.

~✦~

Q: Why do so many lawyers have broken noses?

A: From chasing parked ambulances.

~✦~

Q: Why are lawyers like nuclear weapons?

A: If one side has one, the other side has to get one. Once launched, they cannot be recalled. When they land, they screw up everything forever.

~✦~

Q: Why does the bar association prohibit lawyers from having sex with their clients?

A: To prevent clients from being billed twice for the same service.

~✦~

Q: How many accident attorneys does it take to change a light bulb?

A: Three—one to turn the bulb, one to shake him off the ladder, and the third to sue the ladder company.

~✦~

Q: What is a jury?

A: A collection of people brought together for the purpose of deciding which side has hired the better lawyer.

~ + ~

Q: How many lawyer jokes are there?

A: Only three. The rest are true stories.

~ + ~

Q: What's wrong with lawyer jokes?

A: Lawyers don't think they're funny and other people don't think they're jokes.

~ + ~

Q: What do you call 25 skydiving lawyers?
A: Skeet.

~+~

Q: What do you call a lawyer gone bad?
A: Senator.

~+~

Q: What's the difference between a lawyer and an onion?
A: You cry when you cut up an onion.

~+~

Q: What do you call a lawyer with an IQ of 70?
A: Your Honor.

~✦~

Q: What do you throw to a drowning lawyer?
A: His partners.

~✦~

Q: What do you have if three lawyers are buried up to their necks in cement?

A: Not enough cement.

~♦~

Q: What's the difference between a lawyer and a vulture?

A: The lawyer gets frequent flyer miles.

~♦~

Q: What do you get when you cross a bad politician with a crooked lawyer?

A: Chelsea Clinton.

~♦~

Q: If you have a bad lawyer, why get a new one?

A: Changing lawyers is like moving to a different deck chair on the *Titanic.*

~♦~

Q: How does an attorney sleep?

A: First he lies on one side and then on the other.

~♦~

Q: What's different about a lawyer's word processor?

A: No matter which font you select, everything comes out in fine print.

~♦~

Q: What's the difference between a shame and a pity?

A: If a busload of lawyers goes over a cliff, and there are no survivors, that's known as a pity. If there were any empty seats, that's a shame.

~♦~

Q: What's the difference between a lawyer and a leech?

A: When you die, a leech will stop sucking your blood and drop off.

~♦~

Q: You're in a cage with a grizzly bear and a lawyer. You have a gun, but you only two bullets. What do you do?

A: You shoot the lawyer twice, because the grizzly is the least of your problems.

~+~

Q: What do you get for someone who is graduating from law school?

A: A lobotomy.

~+~

Q: How do you stop a lawyer from drowning?
A: Shoot him before he hits the water.

~+~

Lawyers do it with appeal.
Lawyers do it confidentially.
Lawyers do it on a trial basis.
Lawyers do it until justice prevails.
Lawyers do it as long as you can pay them.
Lawyers do it unless it is prohibited by law.

~+~

Supposedly actual answers given by people when asked how they got into an accident:

Coming home I drove into the wrong house and collided with a tree I don't have.

The other car collided with mine without giving any warning of its intentions.

I thought the window was down, but I found out it was up when I put my head through it.

A truck backed through my windshield and into my wife's face.

A pedestrian hit me and went under my car.

The guy was all over the road. I had to swerve a number of times before I hit him.

I pulled away from the side of the road, glanced at my mother-in-law, and headed over an embankment.

In my attempt to kill a fly, I drove into a telephone pole.

I had been shopping for plants all day and was on my way home. As I reached an intersection, a hedge sprang up, obscuring my vision and I did not see the other car.

I had been driving for 40 years when I fell asleep at the wheel and had an accident.

The pedestrian had no idea which way to run, so I ran over him.

I was on my way to the doctor with rear end trouble when my universal joint gave way causing me to have an accident.

As I approached an intersection a sign suddenly appeared in a place where no stop sign had ever appeared before. I was unable to stop in time to avoid the accident.

To avoid hitting the bumper of the car in front, I struck the pedestrian.

My car was legally parked as it backed into the other vehicle.

I told the police that I was not injured, but upon removing my hat, found that I had a fractured skull.

I saw a slow-moving, sad-faced old gentleman as he bounced off the roof of my car.

The indirect cause of the accident was a little guy in a small car with a big mouth.

I was thrown from my car as it left the road. I was later found in a ditch by some stray cows.

The telephone pole was approaching. I was attempting to swerve out of its way when it struck the front of my car.

~+~

How many lawyers does it take to change a light bulb?

- "How many can you afford?"

- It only takes one to change your bulb...to his.

- Two. One to change it and one to keep interrupting by standing up and shouting "Objection!"

- Three. One to do it and two to sue him for malpractice.

- Three. One to turn the bulb, one to shake him off the ladder, and the third to sue the ladder company.

- Three. One to sue the power company for insufficiently supplying power, or negligent failure to prevent the surge that made the bulb burn out in the first place, one to sue the electrician who wired the house, and one to sue the bulb manufacturer.

- Twenty. Eight to argue, one to get a continuance, one to object, one to demur, two to research precedents, one to dictate a letter, one to stipulate, one to depose, one to write interrogatories, two to settle and one to order a secretary to change the bulb.

~+~

You may need a new lawyer if . . .

Your lawyer tells you that his last good case was of Budweiser.

When the prosecutors see your lawyer, they high-five each other.

Your lawyer picks the jury by playing "duck-duck-goose."

Your lawyer tells you that he has never told a lie.

A prison guard is shaving your head.

~ ✦ ~

These question and answers were purportedly taken from actual court records.

Q: "Was it you or your younger brother who was killed in the war?"

~+~

Q: "Did he kill you?"

~+~

Q: "Doctor, how many autopsies have you performed on dead people?" "

A: "All my autopsies are performed on dead people."

~+~

Q: "You were there until the time you left, is that true?"

~♦~

Q: "How many times have you committed suicide?"

~♦~

Q: "How was your first marriage terminated?"
A: "By death."
A: "And by whose death was it terminated?"

~♦~

Q: "Can you describe the individual?"
A: "He was about medium height and had a beard."
Q: "Was this a male or a female?"

~+~

Q: "Were you present when your picture was taken?"

~+~

Q: "How far apart were the vehicles at the time of the collision?"

~+~

Q: "Now doctor, isn't it true that when a person dies in his sleep, in most cases he just passes quietly away and doesn't know anything about it until the next morning?"

~•~

Q: "What happened then?"

A: He told me, he says, "I have to kill you because you can identify me."

Q: "Did he kill you?"

~•~

Q: "The youngest son, the twenty-year-old, how old is he?"

~•~

Q: "She had three children, right?"

A: "Yes."

Q: "How many were boys?"

A: "None."

Q: "Were there any girls?"

~♦~

Q: Were you alone or by yourself?

~♦~

Q: "Were you present in court this morning when you were sworn in?"

~+~

Q: "You say that the stairs went down to the basement?"
A: "Yes."
Q: "And these stairs, did they go up also?"

~+~

Q: "Now then, Mrs. Johnson, how was your first marriage terminated?"
A: "By death."
Q: "And by whose death was it terminated?"

~+~

Q: "Do you know how far pregnant you are now?"

A: "I'll be three months on March 12th."

Q: "Apparently then, the date of conception was around January 12th?"

A: "Yes."

Q: "What were you doing at that time?"

~✦~

Q: "Do you have any children or anything of that kind?"

~✦~

Q: "Was that the same nose you broke as a child?"

~✦~

Q: "You don't know what it was, and you didn't know what it looked like, but can you describe it?"

~ + ~

Q: "Are you married? "
A: "No, I'm divorced."
Q: "And what did your husband do before you divorced him?"
A: "A lot of things I didn't know about."

~ + ~

Q: "Mrs. Jones, is your appearance this morning pursuant to a deposition notice which I sent to your attorney?"
A: "No. This is how I dress when I go to work."

~ + ~

Q: "Now, you have investigated other murders, have you not, where there was a victim?"

~+~

Q: "Doctor did you say he was shot in the woods?"
A: "No, I said he was shot in the lumbar region."

~+~

Q: "Could you see him from where you were standing? "
A: "I could see his head."
Q: "And where was his head?"
A: "Just above his shoulders."

~+~

Q: ". . . any suggestions as to what prevented this from being a murder trial instead of an attempted murder trial?"

A: "The victim lived."

~+~

Q: "Are you sexually active?"
A: "No, I just lie there."

~✦~

Q: "Are you qualified to give a urine sample?"
A: "Yes, I have been since early childhood."

~✦~

Q: "Have you lived in this town all your life?"
A: "Not yet."

~+~

A Texas attorney, realizing he was on the verge of unleashing a stupid question, interrupted himself and said, "Your Honor, I'd like to strike the next question."

~+~

Q: Do you recall approximately the time that you examined that body of Mr. Huntington at St. Mary's Hospital?

A: It was in the evening. The autopsy started about 5:30 P.M.

Q: And Mr. Huntington was dead at the time, is that correct?

A: No, you idiot, he was sitting on the table wondering why I was performing an autopsy on him!

~＊~

Did you hear about the lawyer hurt in an accident?
An ambulance stopped suddenly.

~＊~

Isn't it a shame how 99% of the lawyers give the whole profession a bad name.

~♦~

If a lawyer and an IRS agent were both drowning, and you could only save one of them . . . would you go to lunch or read the paper?

~♦~

CHAPTER THREE

Here

Comes the Judge…

— HUMOR OFF THE BENCH

A JUDGE WAS ANNOYED TO find that his car wouldn't start. He called a taxi, and soon one arrived at his house.

Climbing in, he told the driver to take him to the halls of justice. "Where are they," asked the driver.

"You mean to say that you don't know where the courthouse is?" asked the incredulous judge.

"The courthouse? Of course I know where that is." replied the driver. "But I thought you said you wanted to go to the 'halls of justice.'"

While questioning a panel for prospective jury members, the lawyer began to fire off questions in the manner of an intimidating showman. As he was finishing up his questioning, he asked, "Do any of you here today dislike lawyers?"

Before the pause became too long, the judge announced, "I do."

~+~

A motorist was hauled before the judge for driving with expired license plates. The judge listened attentively while the motorist gave him a long, plausible explanation.

The judge then said with great courtesy, "My dear sir, we are not blaming you—we're just fining you."

~+~

An English barrister was famed for his dry wit. At the close of one particularly lengthy and convoluted case, the judge, whom the barrister regarded as rather dim, remarked that many of the issues at stake were no longer clear. The barrister then launched into a concise but very lucid account of each of the issues and their ramifications.

"I'm sorry," the judge declared, "but I regret that I am none the wiser."

"Possibly, My Lord," the barrister replied, "but you are better informed."

~♦~

A New York man was forced to take a day off from work to appear for a minor traffic summons. He grew increasingly restless as he waited hour after endless hour for his case to be heard.

When his name was called late in the afternoon, he stood before the judge, only to hear that court would be adjourned for the day and he would have to return the next day.

"What for?" he snapped at the judge.

His honor, equally irked by a tedious day and sharp query roared, "You are in contempt of court, that will be $50.00."

Then, noticing the man checking his wallet, the judge relented. "That's all right. You don't have to pay now."

The man replied, "I'm just seeing if I have enough for two more words."

~✦~

One day in court, a lawyer fell into a heated argument with the presiding magistrate over a point of law. "You've been showing contempt for this court!" the judge finally exclaimed.

"No, Your Honor," the lawyer replied, "I've been trying to conceal it."

~✦~

A judge called two opposing attorneys into his chambers and said, "I have been presented, by both of you, with a bribe."

Both lawyers squirmed uncomfortably. "You, attorney Anderson, gave me $15,000. And you, attorney Johnson, gave me $10,000."

The judge reached into his pocket and pulled out a check. He handed it to attorney Anderson and said, "Now then, I'm returning $5,000, and we're going to decide this case solely on its merits."

~✦~

During a political corruption trial, the prosecuting attorney attacked a witness. "Isn't it true," he bellowed, "that you accepted ten thousand dollars to compromise this case?"

The witness stared out the window as though he hadn't hear the question.

"Isn't it true that you accepted ten thousand dollars to compromise this case?" the attorney repeated.

The witness still did not respond.

Finally, the judge leaned over and said, "Sir, please answer the question."

"Oh," the startled witness said, "I'm sorry, I thought he was talking to you."

~✦~

A new law clerk was asked to prepare a suggested opinion in an important case. After working on the assignment for some time, he proudly handed in a 23-page document.

When he got it back, he found a terse comment in the judge's handwriting on page 7: "Stop romancing—propose already."

~✦~

The presiding judge of a court invited a newly elected judge over for dinner. During the meal, the new judge, a man named Thorn, couldn't help noticing how attractive and shapely the presiding judge's housekeeper was. Over the course of the evening he started to wonder if there was more between the presiding judge and the housekeeper than met the eye. Reading the new judge's thoughts, the presiding judge volunteered, "I know what you must be thinking, but I assure you, my relationship with my housekeeper is purely a professional one."

About a week later the housekeeper came to the presiding judge and said, "Your Honor, ever since that new judge came to dinner, I've been unable to find that beautiful silver gravy ladle. You don't suppose he took it, do you?"

The presiding judge said, "Well, I doubt it, but I'll write him a letter just to be sure." So he sat down and wrote: "Dear Judge Thorn, I'm not saying that you did take a gravy ladle from my house, and I'm not saying you didn't take a gravy ladle. But the fact remains that one has been missing ever since you were here for dinner."

Several days later the presiding judge received a reply letter from Judge Thorn: "Dear Presiding Judge, I'm not saying that you do sleep with your housekeeper, and I'm not saying that you don't sleep with your housekeeper. But the fact remains that if you were sleeping in your own bed, you would have found the gravy ladle by now."

~♦~

A recently appointed district court judge was nervous about presiding impartially over his first criminal trial. As a former prosecutor, he could see the preponderance of evidence was clearly against the defendant. The proceedings went smoothly, until it was time for him to instruct the jury. "The jury," he began, "will be escorted to the guilty room."

~♦~

There are two kinds of lawyers: those who know the law and those who know the judge.

~♦~

A judge, bored and frustrated by a lawyer's tedious arguments, had made numerous rulings to speed the trial along. The attorney had bristled at the judge's orders, and their tempers grew hot. Finally, frustrated with another repetition of arguments he had heard many times before, the judge pointed to his ear and said, "Counselor, you should be aware that at this point, what you are saying is just going in one ear and out the other."

"Your honor," replied the lawyer, "That goes without saying. What is there to prevent it?"

~✦~

A woman was being questioned in a court trial involving slander. "Please repeat the slanderous statements you heard, exactly as you heard them," instructed the lawyer.

The witness hesitated. "But they are unfit for any respectable person to hear," she protested.

"Then," said the attorney, "just whisper them to the judge."

~✦~

"You are a cheat!" shouted the attorney to his opponent.

"And you're a liar!" bellowed the opposition.

Banging his gavel loudly, the judge said, "Now that both attorneys have been identified for the record, let's get on with the case."

~✦~

Prisoner: All I want is justice!

Judge: I'd like to help you, but all I can give you is ten years.

~✦~

During a trial, an elderly English barrister challenged the judge on a point of law. "Sir," the judge declared, "you have grown so old you have forgotten the law."

"I have forgotten more law than you ever knew," the barrister retorted, "but allow me to say, I have not forgotten much."

~✦~

At the start of an important trial, a small town attorney called his first witness to the stand. She seemed like a sweet, elderly woman. He approached her and asked, "Mrs. Jones, do you know me?"

She responded, "Why, yes, I do know you Mr. Williams. I've known you since you were a young boy. You've become a huge disappointment to me. You lie, you cheat on your wife, you manipulate people and talk about them behind their backs. You think you're a hot shot lawyer, when you haven't the brains to realize you never will amount to anything more than a two-bit paper pusher. Yes, I know you."

The lawyer was stunned. Not knowing what else to do he pointed across the room and asked, "Mrs. Jones, do you know the defense attorney?"

She replied, "Why, of course I do. I've known Mr. Bradley since he was a youngster, too. I used to baby-sit him for his parents. And he, also, is a real disappointment. He's lazy, bigoted, never has a nice word to say about anybody, and he drinks like a fish. He's been divorced five times, and everybody knows that his law practice is one of the shoddiest in the entire state. Yes, I know him."

The judge rapped his gavel, to quiet the tittering among the spectators in the courtroom. Once the room was silent, he called both attorneys to his bench. In a quiet, menacing voice, he warned, "If either of you asks her if she knows me, you'll be jailed for contempt!"

~+~

A judge was sentencing criminal defendants when he saw a vaguely familiar face. The judge reviewed his record and found that the man was a career criminal, except for a five-year period in which there were no convictions. "Sir," the judge asked, puzzled, "how is it you were able to stay out of trouble for those five years?"

"I was in prison," he answered. "You should know that—you were the one who sent me there."

"That's not possible," the judge replied, "I wasn't even a judge then."

"No, you weren't the judge," the defendant countered. "You were my lawyer."

~♦~

A judge when being offered a hard-boiled egg as evidence during a trial ordered the egg destroyed by issuing the following:

"No fan I am
Of the egg at hand.
Just like no ham
On the kosher plan.
This egg will rot
I kid you not.
And stink it can
This egg at hand.
There will be no eggs at court
To prove a clog in your 'aort.'

There will be no eggs accepted.
Objections all will be rejected.
From this day forth
This court will ban
hard-boiled eggs of any brand.
And if you should not understand
The meaning of the ban at hand
Then you should contact either Dan,
the Deputy Clerk, or my clerk Jan.
I do not like eggs in the file.
I do not like them in any style.
I will not take them fried or boiled.
I will not take them poached or broiled.
I will not take them soft or scrambled
Despite an argument well-rambled.
No fan I am
Of the egg at hand.
Destroy that egg!
Today! Today!
Today I say! Without delay!"

~✦~

Dissent by Judge Michael Musmanno in a case upholding First Amendment protection to Henry Miller's *Tropic of Cancer* (not written as intended to be humor, but you be the judge):

'Cancer' is not a book. It is a cesspool, an open sewer, a pit of putrefaction, a slimy gathering of all that is rotten in the debris of human depravity. And in the center of all this waste and stench, besmearing himself with its foulest defilement, splashes, leaps, cavorts, and wallows a bifurcated specimen that responds to the name of Henry Miller. One wonders how the human species could have produced so lecherous, blasphemous, disgusting, and amoral a human being as Henry Miller. One wonders why he is received in polite society . . .

Policemen, hunters, constables, and foresters could easily and quickly kill a thousand rattlesnakes but the lice, lizards, maggots, and gangrenous roaches scurrying out from beneath the covers of *The Tropic of Cancer* will enter into the playground, the study desks, the cloistered confines of children and immature minds to eat away moral resistance and wreak damage and harm which may blight countless lives for years and decades to come....

To say that 'Cancer' has no social importance is like saying that a gorilla at a lawn party picnic does not contribute to the happiness of the occasion . . .

The defendant would have reason to say that 'Cancer' is not hard-core pornography; it is, in fact, rotten-core pornography. No decomposed apple falling apart because of its rotten core could be more nauseating as an edible than 'Cancer' is sickening as food for the ordinary mind. 'Cancer' is dirt for dirt's sake, or, more appropriately, as Justice Frankfurter put it, dirt for money's sake. . . .

Then the defendants say that 'Cancer' is entitled to immunity under the First Amendment because court decisions have declared that only worthless trash may be proscribed as obscene. To say that 'Cancer' is worthless trash is to pay it a compliment. 'Cancer' is the sweepings of the Augean stables, the stagnant bilge of the slimiest mudscow, the putrescent corruption of the most noisome dump pile, the dreggiest filth in the deepest morass of putrefaction.

— Commonwealth v. Robin, 218 A.2d 546 (Pa. 1966).

~✦~

Here Judge Musmanno intended to be amusing. A negligence case was brought against the caterer of a diner-dance by a man who slipped on a stalk of asparagus that a waiter had dropped on the dance floor:

The trial judge, an ex-veteran congressman and thus a habitue of formal parties and accordingly an expert in proper wearing apparel at such functions, all of which he announced from the bench, allowed testimony as to the raiment worn by the banquetters. All the men were attired in tuxedos, the pants of which were not mounted with cuffs which could transport asparagus and sauce to the dance floor, unwittingly to lubricate its polished surface. Ruling out the cuffs of the tuxedo pants as transporters of the asparagus, the judge suggested the asparagus, with its accompanying sauce, could have been conveyed to the dance floor by 'women's apparel, on men's coats or sleeves, or by a guest as he table-hopped.'

The Judge's conclusions are as far-fetched as going to Holland for hollandaise sauce. There was no evidence in the case that anybody table-hopped; it is absurd to assume that a man's coat or sleeve could scoop up enough asparagus and sauce to inundate a dance floor to the extent of a three-foot circumference; and it is bizarre to conjecture that a woman's dress without pockets and without excessive material could latch on to such a quantity of asparagus, carry it 20 feet (the distance from the tables to the dance floor), and still have enough dangling to her habiliments to cover the floor to such a depth as to fell a 185-pound gentleman with 35 years' dancing experience who had never before been tackled or grounded while shuffling the light fantastic . . .

It can be stated as an incontrovertible legal proposition that anyone attending a dinner dance has the inalienable right to expect that, if asparagus is to be served, it will be served on the dinner table and not on the dance floor . . .

Judgment reversed with a procedendo.

~+~

CHAPTER FOUR

"Woe Unto Ye Also, Ye Lawyers"

— QUOTATIONS ABOUT LAWYERS AND JUDGES

T HE FIRST THING WE do, let's kill all the lawyers.
Shakespeare, King Henry VI Part 2.

It is the trade of lawyers to question everything, yield nothing, and talk by the hour.
Thomas Jefferson

~✦~

I learned law so well, the day I graduated I sued the college, won the case, and got my tuition back.

Fred Allen

~+~

LAWYER, *n*. One skilled in circumvention of the law.

Ambrose Bierce, *The Devil's Dictionary*

~+~

Make crime pay. Become a lawyer.

Will Rogers

~+~

A lawyer with a briefcase can steal more than a thousand men with guns.

Mario Puzo

~♦~

It is better to be a mouse in a cat's mouth than a man in a lawyer's hands.

Spanish Proverb

~♦~

Woe unto you also, ye lawyers! for ye lade men with burdens grievous to be borne.

The Bible, Luke 11. 46

~♦~

I don't think you can make a lawyer honest by an act of legislature. You've got to work on his conscience. And his lack of conscience is what makes him a lawyer.

Will Rogers

~•~

It is interesting to note that criminals have multiplied of late, and lawyers have also; but I repeat myself.

Mark Twain

~•~

Our wrangling lawyers . . . are so litigious and busy here on earth, that I think they will plead their clients' causes hereafter, some of them in hell.

Robert Burton

~•~

LITIGATION, *n.* A machine which you go into as a pig and come out of as a sausage.

Ambrose Bierce, *The Devil's Dictionary*

~✦~

The only thing a lawyer won't question is the legitimacy of his mother.

W.C. Fields

~✦~

He is no lawyer who cannot take two sides.

Charles Lamb

~✦~

The power of the lawyer is in the uncertainty of the law.

Jeremy Bentham

~+~

I busted a mirror and got seven years' bad luck, but my lawyer thinks he can get me five.

Stephen Wright

~+~

He who is his own lawyer has a fool for a client.

Proverb

~+~

A jury consists of twelve persons chosen to decide who has the better lawyer.

Robert Frost

~+~

Lawyer: One who protects us from robbers by taking away the temptation.

H. L. Mencken

~+~

Baseball is almost the only orderly thing in a very unorderly world. If you get three strikes, even the best lawyer in the world can't get you off.

Bill Veeck

~+~

I haven't committed a crime. What I did was fail to comply with the law.

David Dinkins

~ + ~

The minute you read something that you can't understand, you can almost be sure that it was drawn up by a lawyer.

Will Rogers

~ + ~

If the laws could speak for themselves, they would complain of the lawyers in the first place.

Lord Halifax

~ + ~

The real reason that we can't have the Ten Commandments in a courthouse: You cannot post "Thou shalt not steal," Thou shalt not commit adultery" and "Thou shalt not lie" in a building full of lawyers, judges, and politicians. It creates a hostile work environment.

George Carlin

~♦~

If half the lawyers would become plumbers, two of man's biggest problems would be solved.

Felton Davis, Jr.

~♦~

Ad infinitum: Latin for forever, without limit, indefinitely as in, how long the lawyer intends to keep billing you.

Source unknown

~♦~

I think we may class the lawyer in the natural history of monsters.

John Keats

~ ✦ ~

A lawyer will do anything to win a case, sometimes he will even tell the truth.

Patrick Murray

~ ✦ ~

We all know here that the law is the most powerful of schools for the imagination. No poet ever interpreted nature as freely as a lawyer interprets the truth.

Jean Giraudoux

~ ✦ ~

The average lawyer is essentially a mechanic who works with a pen instead of a ball peen hammer.

Robert Schmitt

~+~

Going to trial with a lawyer who considers your whole lifestyle a Crime in Progress is not a happy prospect.

Hunter S. Thompson

~+~

A lawyer starts life giving $500 worth of law for $5, and ends giving $5 worth for $500.

Benjamin H. Brewster

~+~

A lawyer is a learned gentleman who rescues your estate from your enemies and keeps it himself.

Henry Peter Brougham

~♦~

Bankruptcy: Formal condition of a person being deemed insolvent under law, often encountered by people after paying their lawyer's bill. By declaring bankruptcy, the person agrees to divert his or her remaining assets to the lawyer handling the bankruptcy.

Source unknown

~♦~

And God said: 'Let there be Satan, so people don't blame everything on me. And let there be lawyers, so people don't blame everything on Satan'.

George Burns

~♦~

"You are old," said the youth, "and your jaws are too weak for anything tougher than suet; yet you finished the goose, with the bones and the beak. Pray, how did you do it?" "In my youth," said his father, "I took to the law, and argued each case with my wife and the muscular strength which it gave to my jaw has lasted the rest of my life."

Lewis Carroll

~ + ~

The trouble with law is lawyers.

Clarence Darrow

~ + ~

The lawyer's truth is not Truth, but consistency or a consistent expediency.

Henry David Thoreau

~ + ~

People are getting smarter nowadays; they are letting lawyers, instead of their conscience, be their guide.

Will Rogers

~•~

Felony: Serious crime punishable by having a lawyer represent you.

Source unknown

~•~

LITIGANT, *n.* A person about to give up his skin for the hope of retaining his bones.

Ambrose Bierce, *The Devil's Dictionary*

~•~

Lawyers spend a great deal of their time shoveling smoke.

Oliver Wendell Holmes Jr.

~+~

Lawyers are like rhinoceroses: thick skinned, short-sighted, and always ready to charge.

David Mellor

~+~

Burden of proof: The requirement demanded by lawyers that their clients prove beyond a reasonable doubt that they have absolutely no more money left in their bank accounts. Once the stringent burden of proof requirement is met, confirming that you're flat broke, the lawyer feels ethically compelled to withdraw from your case.

Source unknown

~+~

Scrimgeour: Are you planning to pursue a career in magical law, Miss Granger?

Hermione: No, I actually plan to do some good in the world.

J. K. Rowlins, *Harry Potter And The Deathly Hallows*

~♦~

An incompetent attorney can delay a trial for months or years. A competent attorney can delay one even longer.

Evelle Younger

~♦~

Anybody who thinks talk is cheap should get some legal advice.

Franklin P. Jones

~♦~

You cannot live without the lawyers, and certainly you cannot die without them.

Joseph H. Choate

~✦~

A man who never graduated from school might steal from a freight car. But a man who attends college and graduates as a lawyer might steal the whole railroad.

Theodore Roosevelt

~♦~

In tribal times, there were the medicine men. In the Middle Ages, there were the priests. Today, there are the lawyers. For every age, a group of bright boys, learned in their trades and jealous of their learning, blend technical competence with plain and fancy hocus-pocus to make themselves masters of their fellow men. For every age, a pseudo-intellectual autocracy, guarding the tricks of the trade from the uninitiated, and running, after its own pattern, the civilization of its day.

Fred Rodell

~♦~

"I don't like lawyers, Nannie."
"No one likes lawyers, little boy."

J. P. Donleavy

~♦~

The world has its fling at lawyers sometimes, but its very denial is an admission. It feels, what I believe to be the truth, that of all secular professions this has the highest standards.

Oliver Wendell Holmes, Jr.

~+~

In cross examination, as in fishing, nothing is more ungainly than a fisherman pulled into the water by his catch.

Louis Nizer

~+~

If there were no bad people, there would be no good lawyers.

Charles Dickens

~+~

If it weren't for lawyers, we wouldn't need them.

A. K. Griffin

~♦~

JURISPRUDENCE, *n.* The science of converting a client's money into lawyer's fees.

Ambrose Bierce, *The Devil's Dictionary*

~♦~

I would be loath to speak ill of any person who I do not know deserves it, but I am afraid he is an attorney.

Samuel Johnson

~♦~

Necessity knows no law; I know some attorneys of the same.

Benjamin Franklin

~+~

To succeed in the other trades, capacity must be shown; in the law, concealment of it will do.

Mark Twain

~+~

While law is supposed to be a device to serve society, a civilized way of helping the wheels go round without too much friction, it is pretty hard to find a group less concerned with serving society and more concerned with serving themselves than the lawyers.

Fred Rodell

~+~

You're an attorney. It's your duty to lie, conceal, and distort everything, and slander everybody.

Jean Giraudoux

~+~

[During a trial in which Mae West was accused of indecency on stage]

Judge: Miss West, are you trying to show contempt for this court?

Mae West: On the contrary, Your Honor, I was doin' my best to conceal it.

~+~

I'm not an ambulance chaser. I'm usually there before the ambulance.

Melvin Belli

~+~

There is no better way to exercise the imagination than the study of the law. No artist ever interpreted nature as freely as a lawyer interprets the truth.

Jean Giradoux

~✦~

Only lawyers and painters can turn white to black.

Japanese Proverb

~✦~

God wanted to chastise mankind, so he sent lawyers.

Russian Proverb

~✦~

Witness: Individual who swears to tell the truth, the whole truth, and nothing but the truth, and then proceeds to tell the story the way his lawyer instructed him to tell it.

Source unknown

~+~

Lawyers, I suppose, were children once.

Charles Lamb

~+~

It is unfair to believe everything we hear about lawyers. Some of it might not be true.

Gerald F. Lieberman

~+~

Lawyers should not marry other lawyers. This is called inbreeding, from which comes idiot children and other lawyers.

Adam's Rib [film]

~✦~

I get paid for seeing that my clients have every break the law allows. I have knowingly defended a number of guilty men. But the guilty never escape unscathed. My fees are sufficient punishment for anyone.

F. Lee Bailey

~✦~

Legislation: Laws passed by lawyers masquerading as politicians for the benefit of the other lawyers who contributed to the politicians' campaign coffers.

Source unknown

~✦~

There is never a deed so foul that something couldn't be said for the guy; that's why there are lawyers.

Melvin Belli

~✦~

Judge: a law student who marks his own papers.

H. L. Mencken

~✦~

She cried, and the judge wiped her tears with my checkbook.

Tommy Manville

~✦~

PRECEDENT, *n.* In law, a previous decision, rule or practice which, in the absence of a definite statute, has whatever force and authority a judge may choose to give it, thereby greatly simplifying his task of doing as he pleases.

Ambrose Bierce, *The Devil's Dictionary*

~◆~

Criminal court is where bad people are on their best behavior. It's much more dangerous for lawyers and judges in family court, where good people are at their worst.

Richard Dooling

~◆~

Some people try to get out of jury duty by lying. You don't have to lie. Tell the judge the truth. Tell him you'd make a terrific juror because you can spot guilty people.

George Carlin

~◆~

Young lawyers attend the courts, not because they have business there, but because they have no business.

Washington Irving

~✦~

LIAR, *n.* A lawyer with a roving commission.

Ambrose Bierce, *The Devil's Dictionary*

~✦~

A countryman between two lawyers is like a fish between two cats.

Benjamin Franklin
Dictionary

~＊~

Lawyer: One who protects us from robbers by taking away the temptation.

H. L. Mencken

~ ♦ ~

A lawyer's relationship to justice and wisdom is on a par with a piano tuner's relationship to a concert. He neither composes the music, nor interprets it-he merely keeps the machinery running.

Lucille Kellen

~ ♦ ~

We all know here that the law is the most powerful of schools for the imagination. No poet ever interpreted nature as freely as a lawyer interprets the truth.

Jean Giraudoux

~ ♦ ~

CHAPTER FIVE

Trials and Tribulations

— RIDICULOUS LAWSUITS

A VIRGINIA PRISONER WHO WANTED to be removed from prison and placed in a mental institution sued himself, contending that his crime was committed while he was drunk and that was a violation of his religious beliefs. Therefore, he claimed that he had violated his own civil liberties. He sued himself for $5 million and contended that the state should pay as he was incarcerated and therefore without an income.

A San Quentin death row inmate sued California, claiming his civil rights were violated because his packages were sent via UPS rather than the US Postal Service.

~✦~

A New Yorker sued the Subway sandwich chain because he took a bite of a sandwich and found a seven-inch knife baked into the bread. The knife did not cut him and he did not swallow it. The reason he sued was because he became violently ill with "severe stomach issues" for three hours and claimed he caught food poisoning from the handle of the knife which was plastic and, according to the man, filthy.

~♦~

A resident of Minnesota sued magicians David Blaine and David Copperfield, demanding that they reveal their secret magic tricks to him. He sued for 10% of their total income for life. The basis of the plaintiff's suit: the magicians defy the laws of physics, and are thereby using godly powers. The plaintiff sued not just because the magicians are using God's powers, but because he believed that he was God and therefore it was his powers they are stealing.

~♦~

An publicity-happy actress known as "the Kissing Bandit" was arrested at no fewer than nineteen stadiums for rushing onto the field and attempting to kiss various athletes. On one occasion, her attorney presented a 'gravity defense'; the contention that when she leaned over the rail at a stadium, her 60-inch breasts naturally propelled her over the barrier and onto the field.

~ ✦ ~

An inmate sued the state of Oklahoma alleging a violation of his religious freedoms. The plaintiff could not, however, explain how they were violated because the main tenet of his faith was that all its practices were secret.

~ ✦ ~

A California police officer drew what she thought was her Taser from her belt and used it on a suspect in the back of her car. However, the officer had accidentally drawn her gun instead, and the shot hit the suspect in the chest and killed him.

The city sued the Taser manufacturer, arguing that any reasonable officer could mistakenly draw and shoot his or her gun instead of a Taser. The city wanted the full costs of the wrongful death lawsuit, which the man's family filed against the city.

~♦~

An Ohio inmate sued prison authorities for being denied possession of soap on a rope.

~✦~

A woman sued the Victoria's Secret lingerie company for damage to her eye. The damage was caused, the plaintiff claimed, when she was trying on a new thong. The tight fit caused a metal clip to fly off and hit her in the eye.

~✦~

Anheuser-Busch, brewers of Budweiser, ran a series of ads in which two beautiful women come to life in front of two truck drivers. A Michigan man bought a case of the beer and drank it all, but failed to see two women materialize. He sued Anheuser-Busch for false advertising, asking for a sum in excess of $10,000.

~+~

An Israeli woman sued a television station over a weather forecast that predicted fair weather, but it rained. The woman claimed that the forecast caused her to dress lightly, resulting in her catching the flu, missing a week of work, and spending money on medication. She further claimed that the whole incident caused her stress. She sued for $1,000—and won.

~+~

A plaintiff sued Universal Studios, claiming to have suffered extreme fear, mental anguish, and emotional distress due to visiting Universal's Halloween Horror Nights haunted house, which she said was too scary.

~＊~

An Oklahoma inmate sued prison authorities because he was forced to listen to country music.

~＊~

Some family members of Columbine High School shooting victims sued movie and video game companies for $5 billion, in a class action lawsuit. They claimed that if it had not been for such movies as *The Basketball Diaries* and video games such as *Doom, Duke Nukem, Quake, Mortal Kombat, Resident Evil, Mech Warrior, Wolfenstein, Redneck Rampage, Final Fantasy,* and *Nightmare Creatures,* the massacre would not have occurred; therefore, the makers and distributors of the movies and games were partly responsible.

~✦~

A prisoner who filed a lawsuit claiming mental anguish and post-traumatic stress disorder filed the suit while serving a three-year sentence for killing the defendant's dog in a road rage incident. He claimed the incident had caused his suffering.

~+~

A prisoner sued New York State, claiming he lost sleep and suffered headaches and chest pains after being given a "defective haircut" by an unqualified barber.

~+~

A plaintiff sued NBC for $2.5 million, alleging that an episode of *Fear Factor* caused him "suffering, injury, and great pain." Watching contestants eat rats on television made him dizzy and light-headed, causing him to vomit and run into a doorway, he contended.

~✦~

A plaintiff sued Michael Jordan and Nike founder Phil Knight for $832 million. He claimed to suffer defamation, permanent injury, and emotional pain and suffering because people often mistook him for the basketball star. The plaintiff subsequently dropped the case.

~✦~

A prisoner sued because the Nevada State Prison gave him only two stamps a week to mail letters. As a member of the Universal Life Church, he contended that he must send five letters a week as part of his religious regimen, and inmates are not allowed to receive stamps from outside the prison.

~+~

The television show *Jackass* was sued by a Montana plaintiff for plagiarizing his name and for copyright and trademark infringement and defamation of character. In 1997, the plaintiff legally changed his name to Jack Ass in order to raise public awareness about the perils of drunken driving.

~+~

A New York City woman was awarded $14.1 million by a jury after she was hit by a subway train as she lay on the tracks in an apparent suicide attempt. The award was later reduced by one-third because of her comparative negligence.

~+~

A California couple sued the Bally Health Club for loss of consortium and emotional distress for a cyberspace romance on the man's part. The man alleged that he cut his hand on the towel dispenser at the health club and while home recuperating he went to an online dating service and developed a romance with his co-plaintiff.

~+~

An inmate sued the Utah prison system, saying the state prison violated his right to practice his religion by failing to provide him with a "vampire" diet. The plaintiff also alleged that he was denied a conjugal visit with his "vampress" and denied his right to the sacrament of drinking blood.

~✦~

A California nudist sued an event organizer when he burned his feet while doing a fire walk, even after having been warned that the activity might be dangerous.

~✦~

A woman sued a county in Washington after having an auto accident which left her passenger critically injured. The plaintiff alleged that the police should have pulled her off the road prior to the accident because she had been drinking and did not wear a seatbelt.

~♦~

The estate of a woman killed by a drunk driver sued the rental car company in Florida that rented the car involved in the crash to an Irish tourist. The suit contended that the rental car company should have been more careful when renting cars to Irish customers because the Irish are notorious drunks.

~♦~

A Nevada prisoner sued the state because the prison delivered his mail from 9 PM to 10 PM. He claimed the delivery time interfered with his sleeping pattern.

~✦~

The mayor of a Turkish city called Batman sued Warner Brothers Studio and *The Dark Knight* film director Christopher Nolan for using the name without permission.

~✦~

A man went on a shooting spree that left three dead and five injured at the manufacturing plant where he worked. He was killed by the police in a shoot-out. His mother filed for workman's compensation benefits on his behalf, citing his "death by gunfire while he was on the company clock."

~✦~

An inmate sued when he ordered two jars of chunky peanut butter at the Nevada State Prison canteen but only received one jar of the creamy variety.

~✦~

After a plaintiff was served with divorce papers from his unfaithful wife, he sued her for the return of his donor kidney that she had received eight years earlier, or in the alternative, $1.5 million.

~♦~

A prisoner sued because a Nevada State Prison officer destroyed the bras and bikini panties in his cell. The plaintiff contended he was making the women's clothing to be sent as gifts.

~♦~

A German bank robber was arrested after a bank teller, who realized the robber was hard of hearing, tripped an alarm. The robber sued the bank for exploiting his disability.

~✦~

A Los Angeles attorney sued another attorney who had hung a cardboard tombstone in his office that read, "R.I.P. Jerry Garcia." The plaintiff lawyer, a self-confessed Deadhead, alleged this joke caused him "humiliation, mental anguish, and emotional and physical distress" after seeing the sign. He further added that he had suffered unspecified injuries to his mind and body.

~✦~

A woman golfer hit a shot that ricocheted off railroad tracks that ran through the golf course; the ball hit her in the nose. She was awarded $40,000 in damages because the golf course had a "free lift" rule that allowed players to toss balls which land near the rails to the other side of the tracks. The woman alleged that because the course allowed a free lift, the golf course, in effect, acknowledged the rails to be a hazard.

~+~

A surfer sued another surfer for "taking his wave." The case was dismissed because the plaintiff was unable to put a price on the pain and suffering endured by watching someone ride the wave that was "intended" for him.

~+~

A minister and his wife sued a guide-dog school after a blind man learning to use a seeing-eye dog stepped on the woman's toe.

~✦~

A college student who "mooned" someone from his fourth-story dormitory room window lost his balance, fell out of the window, and injured himself. The student then sued the college for not warning him of the dangers of living on the fourth floor.

~✦~

A woman driving a car collided with a man who was driving a snowmobile. The man was killed in the accident, but since his snowmobile had suddenly cut in front of the car driver, authorities did not charge her. The woman then sued the man's estate for crippling psychological injuries that she claimed she suffered from watching the man die.

~✦~

An author was sued for $60 million dollars after writing a book about a convicted serial killer. Although the inmate was on death row, he claimed that he was innocent in all 16 murders, so that being characterized as a serial killer was false, misleading, and "defamed his good name." He contended that the "falsehoods" would cause him to be "shunned by society and unable to find decent employment" once he returned to private life. [The case was dismissed, but not before $30,000 in legal fees were incurred by the author and his publisher.]

~✦~

A woman who had asked a friend for a haircut was unhappy with the result. She sued her friend for $75,000 alleging that her friend had willfully, intentionally, and maliciously cut her hair without her consent.

~♦~

A convicted bank robber on parole told a bank teller, "Give me the money. I've got a bomb." The bank teller did as instructed, except that hidden in the rolls of money turned over to the robber was an anti-robbery device that released tear gas. The device functioned as intended, prompting the robber to sue the bank for assault.

~♦~

A plaintiff received $780,000 after breaking her ankle tripping over a toddler who was running inside a furniture store. The child was her own son.

~ ♦ ~

A plaintiff won $74,000 and medical expenses when his neighbor ran over his hand with a car. The plaintiff was attempting to steal the car's hubcaps at the time.

~ ♦ ~

A robber was trapped in the garage of a house he had just burglarized. The house's owners were on vacation, and so the robber was locked in the garage for eight days, surviving on a case of Pepsi and a large bag of dry dog food. He sued the homeowner's insurance company for undue mental anguish — and was awarded $500,000.

~+~

A plaintiff was awarded $14,500 and medical expenses after being bitten on the buttocks by his next-door neighbor's beagle that was on a chain in the neighbor's fenced yard. The award was less than sought because the jury felt the dog might have been provoked, since the plaintiff had shot it repeatedly with a pellet gun.

~+~

A jury awarded a woman $113,500 after she slipped on a puddle in a restaurant and broke a bone in her spine. The floor was wet because the plaintiff had thrown soda at her boyfriend during an argument.

~✦~

A woman was awarded $12,000 and dental expenses after she fell from a night club bathroom window to the ground and knocked out two of her front teeth. The plaintiff had been trying to sneak through the ladies' room window to avoid paying a $3.50 cover charge.

~✦~

A man who bought a Winnebago motorhome drove it home on a freeway. He set the cruise control at 70 mph, left the driver's seat, and walked to the back of the motorhome to make a cup of coffee. The Winnebago left the road, crashed, and overturned. The man sued Winnebago for not warning him in the owner's manual that he could not leave the controls unattended. A jury awarded him $1,750,000 plus a new motor home. [Winnebago then added to the owner's manual a warning that cruise control cannot actually drive the vehicle itself.]

~✦~

A man who alleged that his employer discriminated against him was awarded more than $300,000. However, during the trial and before the verdict he held up a convenience store with a shotgun and received a 10-year sentence.

~✦~

A young woman who was driving while under the influence drove her Honda into Galveston Bay in Texas and, too drunk to be able to unfasten her seat belt, drowned. The driver's parents sued Honda for manufacturing a seat belt that cannot be easily unbuckled by a drunk driver who is under water.

~♦~

A concert-goer at Jack Murphy Stadium in San Diego confronted with the stadium's unisex bathroom policy alleged that the presence of women in all the bathrooms embarrassed him and that his emotional distress prevented him from being able to relieve himself. He sued the stadium and the city for $5.4 million, but the case was dismissed.

~♦~

A South Carolina inmate, Jonathan Lee Riches, has filed more than 1,000 frivolous lawsuits, including:

- a suit against baseball player Barry Bonds for $42 million for, among other things, selling steroids to nuns, giving mustard gas to Saddam Hussein, and bench-pressing Riches "to show off in front of his ball park buddies." Hank Aaron's bat, which Riches claimed Bonds used to crack the Liberty Bell, was also named as a defendant in the suit.

- a suit against Elvis Presley for stealing Riches' sideburns and selling him tainted poultry, as well as being in cahoots with Osama Bin Laden.

- a suit against rap producer Suge Knight alleging that the defendant hung him from a Econo Lodge balcony with Vanilla Ice and that Michael Jackson's Neverland Ranch harbors Hitler's army.

- Suing rapper 50 Cents for $35 billion, charging that the musician stole his lyrics and forced him to harass the music groups Bananarama and Tears for Fears. The lawsuit alleged that Riches' plaintiff was a model and actor who has starred in movies like *The Karate Kid, Pee Wee's Big Adventure*, and the Paris Hilton sex tape.

In March 2006, Riches sued 57 pages' worth of defendants—including President George W. Bush, Pope Benedict XVI, Bill Gates, Queen Elizabeth, the Gambino crime family, Three Mile Island, Burt Reynolds, Google, the Salvation Army, the Wu-Tang Clan, the Magna Carta, "tsunami victims," the Kremlin, Nostradamus, the Lincoln Memorial, Nordic gods, Pizza Hut, the European Union, the Methodist Church, Viagra, "ninja samurai fighters," and the planet Pluto—for an unspecified dollar amount for an unspecified civil rights offense.

~✦~

CHAPTER SIX

Sliding Down a Barrister

— LAWYER ANECDOTES

FOLLOWING ONE OF GEORGE Ade's legendary after-dinner speeches, a noted lawyer rose and sardonically asked: "Doesn't it strike the company as a little odd that a professional humorist should be funny?"

Ade, noting that the man's hands were buried deeply in his trouser pockets, replied: "Doesn't it strike the company as a little odd that a lawyer should have his hands in his own pockets!?"

A group of Supreme Court justices once took an outing by boat as a break from the pressures of the law. Justice Benjamin Cardozo, well known for his courtroom dispassionateness, began to feel seasick. A colleague, noticing his discomfort, hurried over to him and asked whether there was anything he could do.

"Yes," replied the judge, "overrule the motion."

~✦~

Abraham Lincoln was once called in to settle a dispute by two men who had been arguing about the correct proportion of the length of a man's legs to the size of his body. Lincoln, in proper legal fashion, listened with care to both sides before speaking.

This seemed, he said at last, to be a question of considerable significance and—as it had caused much bloodshed in the past and would no doubt do so in the future—it was not without great mental anguish and exertion that he reached his opinion. Nonetheless, he concluded, "it is my opinion, all side issues being swept aside, that a man's lower limbs, in order to preserve harmony of proportion, should be at least long enough to reach from his body to the ground."

~✦~

Joseph Choate once opposed an attorney from Westchester County (a wealthy residential area north of New York City) in a lawsuit in New York. The attorney, in a feeble attempt to belittle Choate, warned the jury not to be taken in by his colleague's "Chesterfieldian urbanity."

Choate, summing up his own arguments, in turn urged the jury not to be taken in by his opponent's "Westchesterfieldian suburbanity."

~✦~

Dorothy Parker was once told that a certain London actress had broken her leg. "How terrible," she declared. "She must have done it sliding down a barrister."

~✦~

One wintry evening, Ulysses S. Grant entered a hotel in Galena, Illinois. Sitting by the fire was a group of lawyers, one of whom glanced up at the weather-beaten Grant. "Here's a stranger, gentlemen," he remarked, "and by the looks of him he's traveled through hell itself to get here."

"That's right," Grant cheerfully replied.

"And how did you find things down there?"

"Just like here," Grant declared, "lawyers all closest to the fire."

~♦~

During a Supreme Court hearing one day, another lawyer demonstrated that Joseph Choate had blatantly contradicted the statements in his brief. "Oh well," Choate replied, unperturbed. "I have learned a great deal about the case since the brief was prepared!"

~✦~

"How can I ever thank you?" gushed a woman to Clarence Darrow, after he had solved her legal troubles.

"My dear woman," Darrow replied, "ever since the Phoenicians invented money there has been only one answer to that question."

~✦~

One day the Irish justice Lord Norbury was asked to contribute to a fund for the funeral of an impoverished Dublin attorney. Norbury asked what amount would be appropriate and was told that no one else had offered more than a shilling.

"A shilling!" Norbury exclaimed. "A shilling to bury an attorney? Why, here's a guinea! Bury one and twenty of the scoundrels!"

[A guinea was a sum of money equal to 21 shillings.]

~♦~

Toward the end of his life, the eminent lawyer Elihu Root was often visited by a young man named Sol M. Linowitz , who would read to him.

One day Root asked Linowitz what he planned to do with his life. "I'm not sure," Linowitz replied. "Maybe I'll be a rabbi or perhaps a lawyer."

"Be a lawyer," Root advised. "A lawyer needs twice as much religion as a rabbi!"

[Linowitz became a lawyer, a diplomat, and the chairman of the Xerox Corporation.]

~✦~

Bob Hope once accepted an invitation to address the American Bar Association. "My being here results from a slight misunderstanding," he began. "I thought I was going to talk to the American BRA Association!"

~ ✦ ~

Much enquiry having been made concerning a gentleman, who had quitted a company where Johnson was, and no information being obtained; at last Johnson observed, that 'he did not care to speak ill of any man behind his back, but he believed the gentleman was an attorney.'

—Boswell's *Life of Samuel Johnson*

~ ✦ ~

Concerned about a legal issue one day, the industrialist Russell Sage consulted his lawyer. "It's an ironclad case," the man declared. "We can't possibly lose."

"Then we won't sue," Sage replied. "That was my opponent's side of the case I gave you."

~ ✦ ~